The Ultimate Guide to Strumming

(Second Edition)

Learn to Strum With Great Technique,
Master the Key Strumming Patterns, and
Discover My Most Exciting Tricks and Techniques

Dan Thorpe

Disclaimer

All the material contained in this book is provided for educational and informational purposes only. No responsibility can be taken for any results or outcomes resulting from the use of this material.

While every attempt has been made to provide information that is both accurate and effective, the author does not assume any responsibility for the accuracy or use/misuse of this information.

Audio and Downloads

You can get the audio for every musical example contained inside this book. As well as that, you can also get a free printable TAB PDF, exclusive bonus content, hidden extras, and other useful strumming goodies, all on this link here—**rockstarpublishing.co.uk/strum**

Free Resources

You can also go to my website, **guitardomination.net** to join the free mailing list and get my best tips, tricks, and freebies sent to your inbox.

The Ultimate Guide to Strumming is the most comprehensive book you will find on how to take your strumming skills to new heights. Inside you will discover a step-by-step method for strumming with great tone and technique, playing the most important strum patterns, and having endless fun with a wide variety of elegant sounding techniques.

Reader reviews for *The Ultimate Guide to Strumming*

Five Stars ★★★★★

"This is the best strumming book I have read! He is an excellent teacher! Puts fun and enjoyment back into learning guitar… a must-buy book! You will not be disappointed!"

—rushcowski

Five Stars ★★★★★

"As an intermediate guitarist, I found this book to have lots of easily implementable strumming ideas that I had been overlooking."

— J. D. Mann

Five Stars ★★★★★

"This book quickly helped me find the holes [in my strumming] and plug some of them. Within a couple of hours, my playing had improved dramatically. It is the sort of book I wish I had read early on when I first started playing."

— Rintu Basu

Table of Contents

Five Stars ★★★★★

"I purchased this book a year ago on Dan's website. Personally, I find it very useful in many ways. I improved my rhythm, and I learned a lot about music theory. Dan is an amazing guitar teacher, his method is easy to follow for everyone no matter how old or young you are."

—Dubravka

Five Stars ★★★★★

"This new version combines all the useful information of his earlier book with all the extremely helpful information I received from his website. In short, it's a great place for any beginner or intermediate to learn important aspects of strumming… you'll be up to playing with a group or solo in no time!"

—Jake

Five Stars ★★★★★

"If there is a more detailed and structured course on strumming I'm yet to find it. Dan's approach builds slowly and surely giving you everything you need to improve your strumming along with audio samples to compare and contrast."

— Amazon Reviewer

INTRODUCTION—YOUR EXCITING STRUMMING JOURNEY!

Strumming is something I often call a "dark art". The reason why is that although all guitarists can strum to a certain level, many struggle to reach the high standards of professional and highly enjoyable strumming.

To me, strumming is summed up perfectly with this wonderful old quote:

"The fretting hand is the brain, and the strumming hand is the soul."

This is so true, and it highlights the fact that the fretting hand does a lot of the technical work (such as playing chords and scales). It is the strumming hand though that brings life and soul to the music. If you have ever heard a guitarist strum some amazing things with just a couple of simple chords, then you will know what I mean.

To be able to strum to a high standard, you need a proper plan for how to fix bad habits, learn the basics, discover the key strumming patterns, and develop all of the above in exciting ways. This book is that guide.

Learning and improving your guitar playing is a journey, and in many ways, it is like learning to drive. So, let's get you moving steadily through the gears and out there cruising down the highway!

Come and join me on an exciting journey of strumming discovery…

How to Work Through This Book

I have split the book into three distinct parts. Ideally, you will work through the book in order. Even though I know some of you will secretly want to skip ahead, please do ensure you have the basics sorted first! Here is a little bit about each section:

Part 1—the fundamentals. Fix your strumming basics once and for all. This section is like learning how to safely control the car, work the clutch, and start driving smoothly.

Part 2—the strumming patterns. Learn the 14 most useful strumming patterns ever. This section is like taking the car out for a spin on the big roads with the wind in your hair!

Part 3—the intermediate techniques. Discover how to add more groove, excitement, and interest to your strumming. This is like the guitarist's equivalent to handbrake turns and driving on two wheels!

The Audio

To make the examples easier to learn, each track has two audio versions. **One is played at a normal speed, and one is played at a slowed down speed.**

Remember, you can get the audio, available to stream or download (as well as some very useful goodies) for every example in the book at the link below:

rockstarpublishing.co.uk/strum

Listen to each track and play along with them when you are ready to. This will help you get the rhythm correct. Play along with the slowed-down versions of the audio before attempting the full speed version.

A Quick Guide to "Tab" and the Strumming Diagrams

Below is a quick primer on reading guitar TAB. If you don't already know, TAB is music notation specific to the guitar. **Each horizontal line represents a string of the guitar and each number represents a fret.** The following image shows a brief guide on how to read TAB, but for a more detailed guide go to…

rockstarpublishing.co.uk/tab

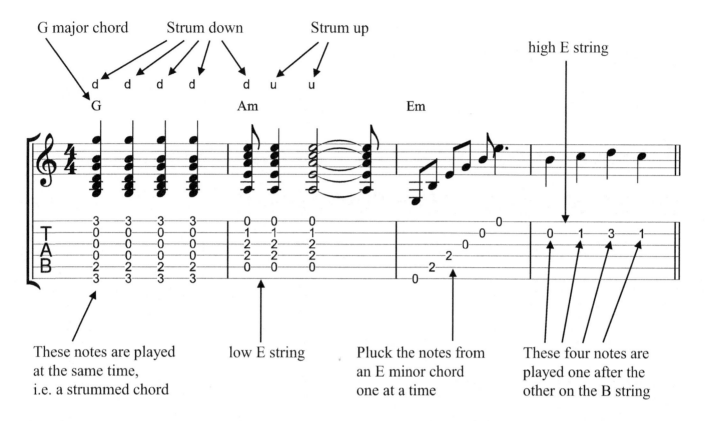

These notes are played at the same time, i.e. a strummed chord

low E string

Pluck the notes from an E minor chord one at a time

These four notes are played one after the other on the B string

In part 2 of the book, you will see strumming diagrams for each of the patterns. These show the recommended **order of down and upstrums ("d" and "u") in relation to the beats in the bar.**

These diagrams are useful but make sure you listen closely to the audio tracks to hear the rhythm of each pattern.

On both the TAB and the strumming diagrams, you will see either an uppercase "D" or lowercase "d".

- Uppercase = strum louder (called an "accent")
- Lowercase = strum at a normal volume

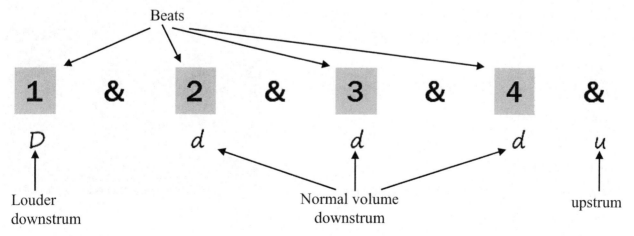

3

PART I:

THE ALL-IMPORTANT FUNDAMENTALS OF BEING A GOOD STRUMMER!

The first thing we need to do before we get to the really exciting stuff is to get the fundamentals sorted. Do not forget there is audio for this book. Aim to play along with the tracks, as doing so will help you get the most out of the book.

Remember, you can download or stream the audio for the book. You can do so at the following link: **rockstarpublishing.co.uk/strum**

Before we begin, here are a few pointers that many guitarists neglect.

Ensure Your Chords are Clear

If your chords buzz or sound muted, it won't matter how well you strum, things will simply not sound great. Here are some tips to help with this:

- Keep your fretting hand nails short.
- Fret the chords using the lightest touch possible. I call this "Minimum Pressure Required".
- Get close to the frets and you will not have to press as hard.
- Regularly check you are not fretting chords with too much pressure.
- Practise on a guitar that is suitable for you.

A lot of the examples in the book are played using super simple chords. This should help if any of your chords buzz. You can practise any of the examples in the book on any chords you are comfortable with as well as the ones taught.

Get Your Capo Ready!

Using a capo can make playing chords easier. Here's why:

- Using a capo means we can play chords higher up the neck where the **frets are closer together** (e.g., the frets are closer together at fret 5 than fret 1).
- This means your fingers do NOT have to stretch as much, making your chords **less likely to buzz** and more comfortable to play. Hooray for the power of a capo!

For this reason, many of the audio examples in the book are played with a capo. Some guitarists prefer not to use one, so feel free to place a capo where you like or to not use one at all. Just be aware, to play along with the audio, you will need to use a capo for many of the examples.

Strumming with Your Pick or Fingers?

When it comes to strumming, I prefer to use a pick, and so do most of my students. This is because strumming can be quite tough on the fingers and nails if you don't use a pick.

When I do strum with my fingers, it is usually when there are strummed passages within a fingerpicked song. Feel free to use a pick or your fingers, but if you are in doubt as to which to use, start with a pick.

In terms of your choice of pick:

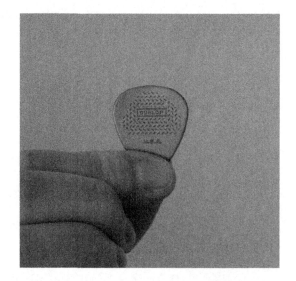

- For strumming, these days I favour <u>nylon picks</u> with a thickness of between **0.5 and 0.73**.
- If you are a beginner, start with a **thinner pick**, as they tend to be easier to strum with.
- Later you can start to move towards a thicker pick, but strumming an acoustic with a pick thicker than 0.73 often doesn't sound that great in my experience.

The Strumming Fundamentals

Let's learn some useful exercises. Each of these will help you build up good strumming habits. These are the exact exercises I have used for years with many private students. They are simple but mighty effective.

The "Pendulum"

When you strum, generally you should aim to move your strumming hand up and down in a steady pendulum-like motion. This will help you to get a good basic strumming movement and rhythm.

Tracks #1-2   *Capo 4—50 bpm*

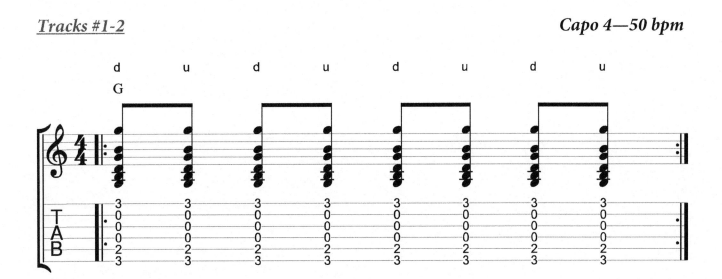

This is how we play the "Pendulum" with a *G Major* chord.

- **Use all down and upstrums** being careful to not miss any strums on the way down or up.
- **Make sure your elbow and wrist** are relaxed and not too rigid as you strum.

- **Don't twist or turn your wrist as you strum.** This can cause you to "drag" your pick/fingers across the strings, causing a harp-like sound.
- **Strum through the strings in a fluid motion.** Imagining the strings are one block and NOT just individual strings can help.

Practise this exercise until you can strum *down and up*, over and over in a fluid way. Repeat until it feels natural and sounds smooth.

Power Tip

Try tapping your foot as you play the downstrums. It can be tricky at first and there will be more tips on this later. For now, give it a go.

Root Note Targeting

A lot of guitarists make the mistake of strumming the wrong strings. This can cause your strumming to sound sloppy. Let's practise strumming from the correct strings for the chords of *C Am G Em D*.

Tracks #3-4   *Capo 4—110 bpm*

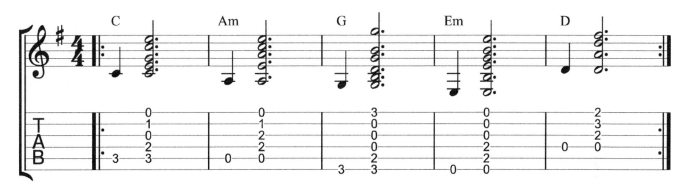

1. **Rest your pick on the "root note" of each chord** (more on the meaning of "root notes" in a moment).
2. **Pause momentarily** before you pluck this string (this is so you can check you are about to pluck the correct string), and then pluck.
3. **Finally, strum the chord** with a relaxed and fluid downstrum.

The aim of this exercise is for you to be able to play the correct root note for each chord as a habit. Once the habit is formed, strumming from the correct string in practice will be easier. Practise this on <u>one chord at a time</u> at first and practise the exercise with all the chords you know too.

Power Tip

The "root note" is the note the chord is named after. E.g., in a *G Major* chord, the root note is the note of G found on the 3rd fret of the low E string. This is the string you pluck or strum from in *a G Major* chord.

Tight Grip Vs. Soft Grip (For Pick Strummers)

Not many guitarists know that how hard you grip the pick affects the tone. A tight grip can make fluid strumming difficult and cause your tone to be loud and brash. This exercise will help you learn what NOT to do as well as what you should do.

Tracks #5-6   *Capo 4—50 bpm*

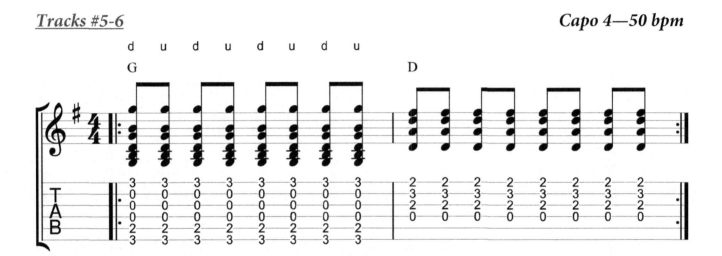

Step 1—What NOT to do!

- Squeeze your pick as **<u>tightly</u>** as you can.
- Now strum with **down and upstrums** (shown by "d" and "u").
- Keep squeezing the pick tightly but strum as quietly as you can.

Most students find this almost impossible. I get students to do this to highlight how strumming can sound so sloppy when gripping the pick too tightly.

Step 2—What you should aim to do!

- Now, grip the pick as **<u>softly</u>** as you can using a super gentle touch.
- Strum as quietly as you can.
- If the tone and feel aren't pleasant, grip it softer until it is.

A good rule of thumb is to use just enough pressure, so the pick doesn't fall out of your fingers, but not much more. If you have done this exercise correctly, you will have found gripping the pick softly gives you a pleasant and mellow tone that is nice to listen to.

By the way, throughout the book, we will be using strumming directions ("d" and "u") for many examples. Only the 1st bar for these examples will show the strumming directions above it. Unless directed otherwise, continue strumming in the same way for any bars that follow.

Showing strumming directions for every bar would make things look a little cluttered and is not really necessary.

Power Tip

Keep adjusting the amount of pressure you use until you get the "sweet spot". This is the point where the pick feels comfortable and your tone is pleasant.

Upstrums Only!

When playing upstrums, many guitarists make the mistake of trying to strum all the strings. Instead, I encourage students to strum *only* the <u>"treble strings"</u> (G, B, and high E strings). This can make strumming upstrums easier and can help them sound more pleasant.

<u>*Tracks #7-8*</u>   *Capo 4—80 bpm*

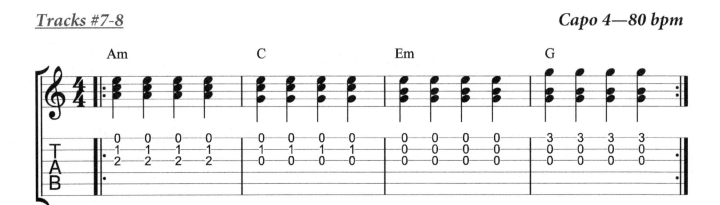

- **Practise *only* strumming upstrums** for this exercise—<u>no downstrums</u>.
- **Strum the three treble strings** (the G, B, and high E strings) in a smooth and fluid motion.

Keep practising your upstrums with the lightest and softest touch possible. After a little while, you will be able to feel and hear them sounding smooth in your real playing.

Power Tip

Don't worry about being too precise. Aim to strum just the 3 treble strings as much as possible, but if you strum 2 or 4 strings with your upstrums, it is not the end of the world.

"Index Vs. Thumb" (For Fingerstyle Strummers)

If you strum with your fingers and NOT a pick, I recommend you use your <u>index finger</u>. Some guitarists like to use their thumb, but it can sound a little quiet and subdued in comparison.

Tracks #9-10   *Capo 4—60 bpm*

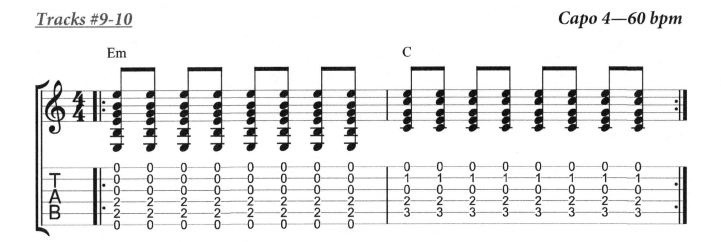

For this exercise, strum everything with all **down and upstrums** again. This is what I recommend you do when strumming with the <u>index finger</u>:

- **Strum with the nail** for downstrums.
- **Strum with the skin side** for upstrums.

In the audio track, the first time the piece is played it is strummed with the index finger. The second time it is strummed with the thumb. Listen to how the index finger gives us a bit of a fuller tone compared to the thumb.

Power Tip

Remember, there are no rules when it comes to learning to play an instrument—only guidelines. If you prefer to strum with your thumb, go for it. However, for those "on the fence", I recommend you use your index finger for strumming.

Root Note Targeting and Upstrums!

Now let's combine the previous exercises. The following three steps will help you both strum from the correct string and play a smooth upstrum in a practical manner.

Tracks #11-12   *Capo 4—100 bpm*

1. **Pluck the root note** of the chord with a down pluck.
2. Next, strum the chord with a **downstrum.**
3. **Finally, strum upwards** ensuring you only strum the treble strings here.

Work on one chord at a time for this exercise and be patient. This is a really good step to master.

Power Tip

There are three basic motions happening here. 1) Root note pluck, 2) a downstrum, 3) a 'treble strings only' upstrum. Do not try to jump from one step to the next too quickly and be as accurate as possible here.

Now that you have gone through the above exercises, don't stop there. Repeat them, and keep coming back to them, even as you work through the book.

Improving your strumming tone is an ongoing process that never ends, so keep working on it every day!

How to Understand Time Signatures Once and For All

Now that we have covered the basics of strumming technique, the next step is to make sure you have a good understanding of time signatures.

A "time signature" tells us how many beats there are in a bar of music. They are the first thing you need to know about a piece of music before you play it. Here we have the three most common time signatures, along with a simple musical example for each. The strumming is basic but practise the examples until they make sense. Doing so will help you understand basic time signatures once and for all.

4/4 Time

Tracks #13-14   *Capo 4—60 bpm*

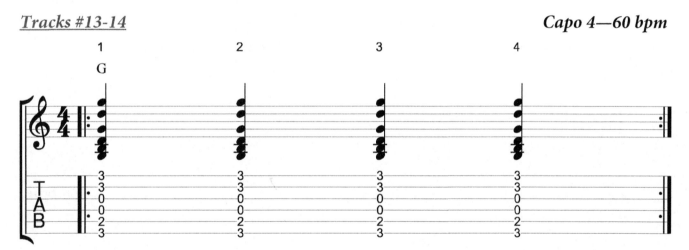

4/4 is the most common time signature in most music—especially in pop, folk, rock, blues, and country music.

- **It features 4 beats per bar**—count them as *"1 2 3 4"* (as shown above the TAB).
- Use all **downstrums** to play this piece.

Notice in the above example, we are playing a different version of *G Major* compared to what we have done so far. This version of *G Major* and the other one as used earlier are both really useful (depending on the situation) so it's a good idea to be able to play both.

15

3/4 Time

Tracks #15-16   _Capo 4—60 bpm_

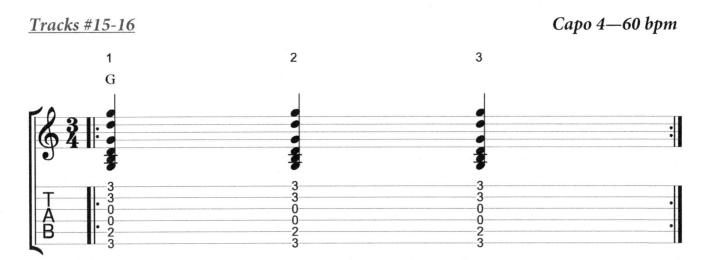

3/4 is often called "waltz" time. A lot of traditional songs, classical pieces, and Christmas carols use this time signature.

- **It features 3 beats per bar**—count them as **_"1 2 3"_**.
- _Use all **downstrums** to play the piece above while you count the beats._

6/8 Time

Tracks #17-18   _Capo 4—60 bpm_

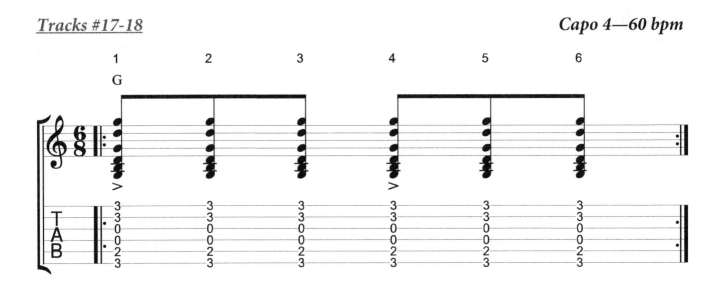

6/8 time is a really nice time signature that is a little different to both 4/4 and 3/4.

- **It features 6 beats per bar**—count them as *"1 2 3 4 5 6"*.

- *Use all **downstrums** to play the piece above while you count the beats.*

- **Accent beats 1 and 4** (meaning strum louder).

The "accent" is key to the sound of this time signature. If you do not accent beats 1 and 4, this time signature can quickly lose its feel.

Listen closely to the audio to hear the above examples in action. Get good at playing these examples. Doing so will help you understand the three most commonly used time signatures in music. Let's move on but come back to this section later on if you need to.

The Essential "Sub-Divisions" of Rhythm

Now it is time to get a good, solid understanding of rhythm. This means learning about "sub-divisions".

A "sub-division" is how a beat is divided up into smaller chunks. Each chunk lasts for a different length of time, and it is the combination of these "chunks" that create the interesting rhythms we hear in music. In this section, you will learn what each sub-division is.

The "American" names for each sub-division are shown first and the "English" names are in brackets. As the American names are easier to understand for many, we will continue using them throughout the rest of the book.

Whole Note (Semi-Breve)

Tracks #19-20   *Capo 4—50 bpm*

Whole notes are very simple, and to play them you strum just once per bar.

- **A whole note** lasts for 1 bar.
- Strum a downstrum on beat 1 letting it ring out for the rest of the bar.
- Try to count the beats of 1, 2, 3, 4 out loud while you do so.

As whole notes last for a whole bar, we don't use them much in strumming apart from as the occasional "ring out" to lead into another section or to end a song.

Half Note (Minim)

Tracks #21-22   *Capo 4—50 bpm*

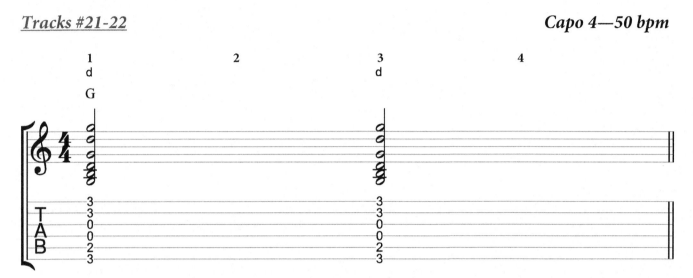

In the TAB and notation above, you will see that the bar is split into two equal, spaced halves—hence the name, "half note".

- **A half note** lasts for half the bar, which is the length of two beats.
- To play a complete bar of half notes, you simply strum **two downstrums** on beats <u>1 and 3</u>.

Just like whole notes, we don't tend to use these much when strumming.

Quarter Note (Crochet)

Tracks #23-24   *Capo 4—50 bpm*

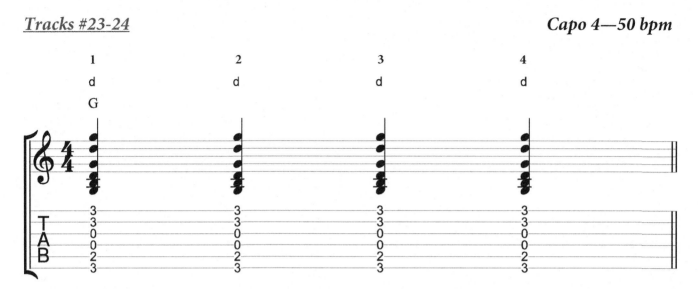

In the TAB and notation above, you will see how the bar is split into quarters for "quarter" notes.

- **A quarter note** lasts for a quarter of a bar, which is the length of one beat.
- To play a complete bar of quarter notes, you simply strum **four downstrums** on beats 1, 2, 3, 4.
- When you strum quarter notes, the notes should be at the same time as a foot tap or the click of a metronome.

Quarter notes are used a lot in music, and most simple strumming patterns use them. Although simple, keep practising these until you are comfortable with them.

Eighth Note (Quaver)

Tracks #25-26   *Capo 4—50 bpm*

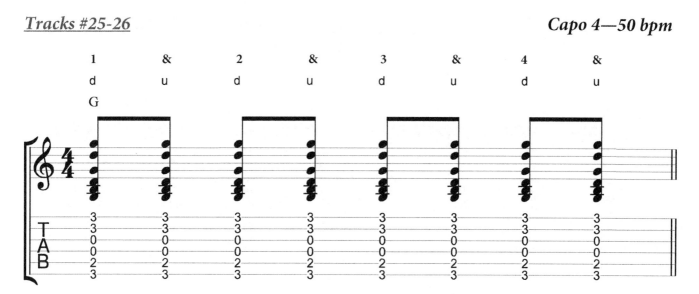

This is where things start to get busier. In the above diagram, you will see that you now need to strum both down and upstrums to play eighth notes.

- **An eighth note** lasts for an eighth of a bar, which is the length of half a beat.
- To play a complete bar of eighth notes, strum eight times on each sub-division of <u>1 & 2 & 3 & 4 &.</u>
- To practise this sub-division strum alternating down and upstrums.
- This means strumming downstrums on the beats of 1, 2, 3, 4, and strum upstrums on the "&" in between the beats.

Most strumming patterns use eighth notes at some point as they are probably the most common sub-division in music. Spend some time practising these as they are super important!

Sixteenth Note (Semi-Quaver)

Tracks #27-28   *Capo 4—50 bpm*

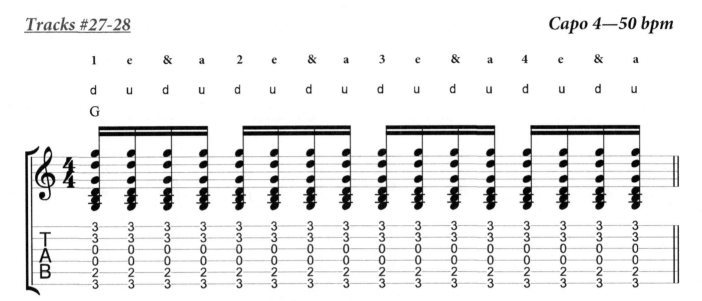

Sixteenth notes are pretty fast and can be very tricky at first. Here are some pointers on this sub-division.

- **A sixteenth note** lasts for a sixteenth of a bar, which is the length of a quarter of a beat.
- To count sixteenth notes, you can no longer count 1 & 2 & 3 & 4 &.
- Instead, count—"1 e and a" and so on, as shown above the TAB—the "e" and the "a" can help you count this sub-division accurately.
- There are 16 strums here and you should try to strum them using alternating **down and upstrums.**
- If you struggle with these at first, try strumming the downstrums on the beats of 1, 2, 3, 4, a little harder than the other strums. This can help you get into the groove for this sub-division easier.

Try playing along with the slowed-down audio track to get the timing correct. If you find sixteenth notes really tough though, leave them for now and come back to this section later on.

Get as comfortable as possible playing and understanding the above sub-divisions. Play along with me in the audio and then when you are ready, let's try this fun game…

The "Strumming 101" Game

This fun exercise is designed to help you combine the above sub-divisions together in a seamless and musical manner.

I take all my students through this, and they find it very helpful. Keep the earlier technical tips in mind as you practise it and try the exercise multiple times. Each chord is being played with a *G Major* **chord with a capo on <u>fret 4</u>**. Simply strum this chord and follow the TAB and notation throughout.

The Setup

Before starting, let's get you set up to play the exercise.

- Begin by counting out loud, *"1 and 2 and 3 and 4 and"*.
- **Tap your foot** every time you say a number, i.e., <u>1 2 3 4</u>.

Don't rush this step and if need be, you can do this for a few minutes to get into the groove.

Step 1

Now, let's start adding some strums…

Tracks #29-30   *Capo 4—60 bpm*

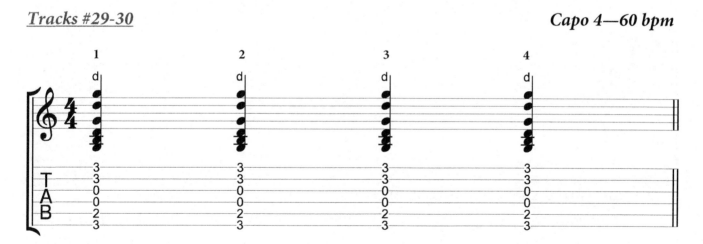

- Keep tapping your foot to the beat and counting out loud *"1 and 2 and 3 and 4 and"*.
- Strum downstrums in time with the foot taps on the beat.

Step 2

Tracks #31-32   *Capo 4—60 bpm*

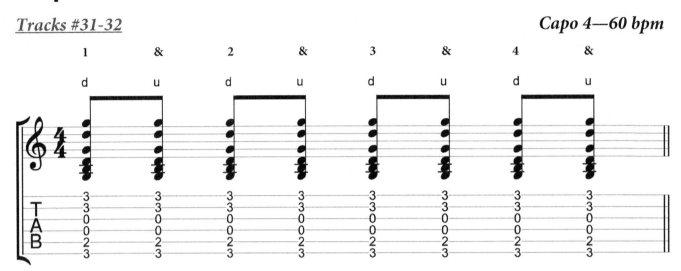

- Keep strumming downstrums on beats 1, 2, 3, 4.
- While doing so, strum upwards in between.
- Try to keep counting out loud and tapping your foot to the beat if you can. (Try again later though if you can't).

Step 3

Tracks #33-34   *Capo 4—60 bpm*

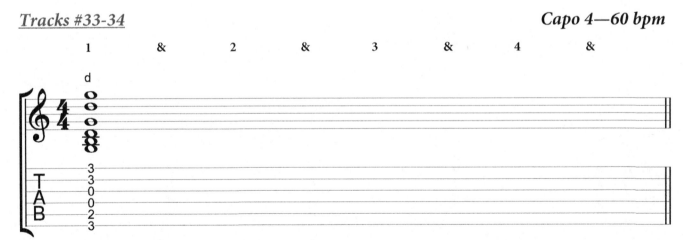

- Now, strum a sole downstrum on beat 1.
- Keep your strumming arm moving in a "pendulum" motion as described earlier (while keeping your foot tapping to the beat).

- This one simple strum can feel strange here, but this step is all about getting you to keep your strumming arm moving like a pendulum!

Step 4

Tracks #35-36   *Capo 4—60 bpm*

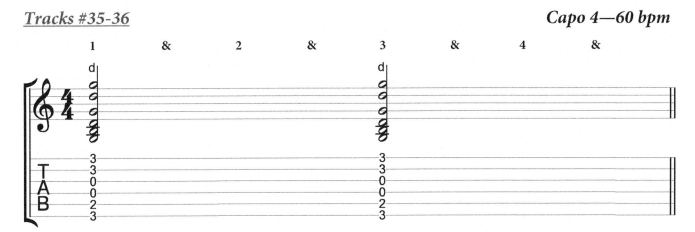

- Strum the two downstrums on beats 1 and 3.
- This is a simple step but try to keep strumming in a "pendulum" motion.
- If you count the beats, it can be more helpful to do so out loud and not in your head.

Step 5

Tracks #37-38   *Capo 4—60 bpm*

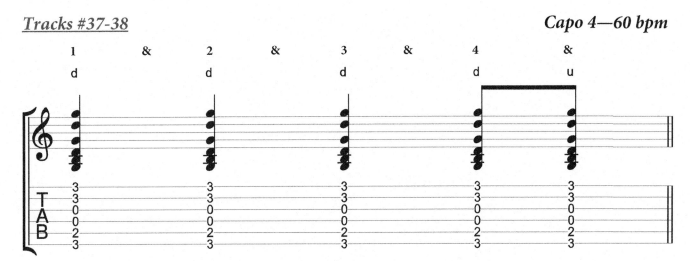

- This is a busier strumming pattern with four downstrums and one upstrum at the end.

- Listen closely to the rhythm and play along with the audio.

Keep practising each of the above steps and then in a moment we will put it all together for the "Strumming 101" game.

Put It All Together and Repeat

Get good at each of the above and then try putting all the steps together *without* stopping. Doing this will help you understand sub-divisions better and will help improve your ability to switch between rhythms.

Below are all the steps we have covered in this section played one after the other. Take a listen to the audio to hear this in action and follow the rhythm closely.

Tracks #39-40   *Capo 4—60 bpm*

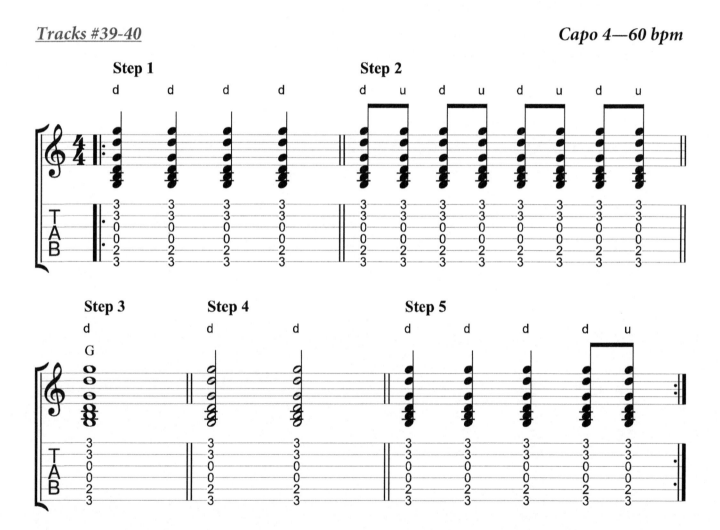

Congratulations and well done if you are able to play the above! If you were not able to right away, do not worry, try again later. Sometimes, just a short break can help things "click".

27

Power Tip

Why is foot-tapping so useful?

I urge you to tap your foot to the beat for all of the examples in this book. The reason why is that foot-tapping can help you keep in time and smoothly mix and match rhythms better. Doing this can also help prevent the dreaded speeding or slowing down issues that plague many beginners.

You may not be able to tap your foot to the beat right away with the examples, as that is tough. Do keep trying though and remember, if you struggle, learn the example without the foot tap for now. Then you can try it again later with the foot tap once you are more comfortable with the strumming pattern or technique.

The Light and Dark of "Bass/Treble" Strumming

Most pros do NOT strum all the strings all the time, and this is something that separates them from amateurs.

If you constantly strum all the strings in a chord, things can sound pretty boring, pretty quickly! For example, you probably know that in a *C Major* chord, you can strum five strings. Although it will not sound bad if you strum all five strings, using a technique called "Bass/Treble" strumming can make things sound more interesting right away! Let's check it out.

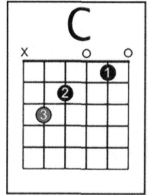

What Is "Bass/Treble" Strumming?

"Bass/Treble" strumming is where we alternate between strumming the:

- **Bass strings** (low E, A, and D strings)
- **Treble strings** (G, B, and high E strings)

You can think of the bass strings and the treble strings as mini "blocks" of strings. Alternating your strumming between these two "blocks" will add more light and dark tones to your strumming, thus giving it more life.

For this technique, I recommend you start by using **downstrums throughout** (as this makes practising the technique easier at first).

29

"Bass/Treble" Strumming Ex. #1

Tracks #41-42   *Capo 4—240 bpm*

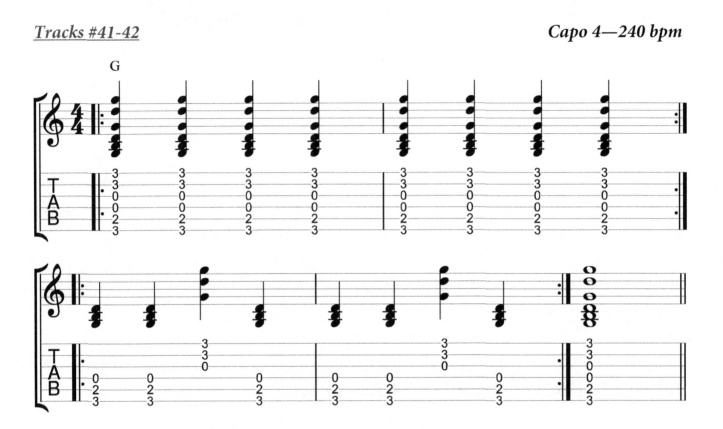

Let's hear the difference between normal strumming and "Bass/Treble" strumming.

- Bars 1 and 2 are strummed normally where **all the strings** are strummed. In the audio these two bars are repeated.
- Strum bar 3 and 4 as—*bass, bass, treble, bass* (repeated).
- Listen to how "Bass/Treble" strumming (bars 3 and 4) sounds more interesting compared to the normal strumming (bars 1 and 2)!

You wouldn't normally switch between normal and "Bass/Treble" strumming every two bars like we are doing here, but this example is there to highlight the difference between the two.

"Bass/Treble" Strumming Ex. #2

Tracks #43-44   *Capo 4—240 bpm*

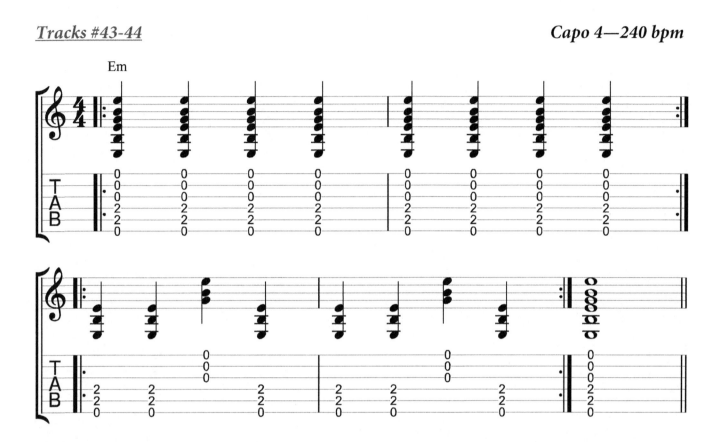

Here we are strumming an *E minor* chord.

- Notice how the "Bass/Treble" bars turn this simple rhythm into something far more interesting.
- Try to keep the strumming hand relaxed and fluid throughout.
- Take your time getting this example accurate and work on it in two halves if you need to.

Remember, it can be easier to use all downstrums with this technique. Aim to get the sound as "tight" as you can.

"Bass/Treble" Strumming Ex. #3

Tracks #45-46   *Capo 4—240 bpm*

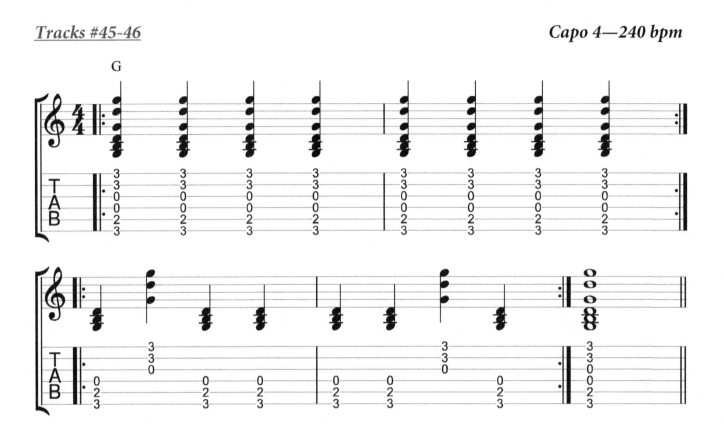

Again, we start off with normal downstrums for bars 1 and 2.

- What is interesting about bars 3 and 4 (the "Bass/Treble" bars) is that they are slightly different to each other.
- Notice, how it starts off ***bass, treble, bass, bass…***
- Then it changes to ***bass, bass, treble, bass.***
- I highly recommend you learn the "Bass/Treble" bars in two parts like this.

That may sound a touch confusing at first but listen closely to the audio to hear how the subtle change creates a really interesting rhythmic shift.

"Bass-Treble" Strumming Ex. #4

Tracks #47-48   *Capo 4—240 bpm*

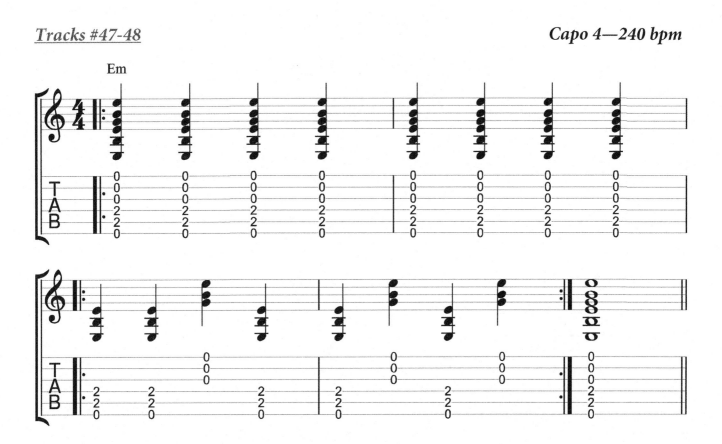

The final example is one I like to use a fair bit.

- Once again you can split bars 3 and 4 up into two halves to learn it faster.
- The contrast between the two halves of the "Bass/Treble" bars gives this pattern lots of character.

This example is not easy, so practise it slowly at first, or you may find yourself tripping up!

One thing I should point out is that for these Bass/Treble examples, although the tempo is at **240 bpm, we are playing quarter notes**. This is the same as playing **eighth notes at 120 bpm.** I have notated it like this purely so you can see in a clearer manner what is happening in the Bass/Treble bars. Listen to the audio to hear the examples in action and don't forget to play along with the slowed down tracks first.

"Bass/Treble" Summary

"Bass/Treble" strumming is NOT an exact science. Try to be precise of course, but do not worry if you strike an extra string here and there. The most important thing to keep in mind with this technique is that the rhythm should be tight, and you should get the overall groove solid.

What is great about "Bass/Treble" strumming is that you can take the most simple and mundane rhythm and give it lots more life by simply changing up how you strum the strings—i.e., utilizing "Bass/Treble" strumming!

You won't use "Bass/Treble" strumming all of the time but a little can go a long way. Keep it in mind for the rest of the book and use it when instructed or just when you think it might be fun to try it out!

Part 1 Summary

Below is a summary of what we've covered in *Part 1*. Use this as a checklist and reference it regularly.

✓ **Make sure your chords are clear**.

✓ Use "Minimum Pressure Required" with your fretting hand.

✓ **If your chords buzz,** keep working on your technique.

✓ Using a capo can help you play chords easier and with less buzzing.

✓ **Keep your strumming arm moving** in a <u>"Pendulum"-like motion</u>. .

✓ **Strum from the correct root note** (e.g., for a *D Major* chord, strum from the D string).

✓ **Upstrums**—aim to smoothly strum the <u>treble strings</u> only.

✓ **Strumming with a** *pick*—use a <u>nice light grip</u> for best results.

✓ **Strumming with your** *fingers*—I recommend you use your <u>index finger</u>.

✓ **Experiment with using different picks** until you find one that suits you (0.5-0.73 are a good thickness to use).

✓ **Always aim to keep a smooth and steady tempo** when strumming.

✓ **The five "sub-divisions"** are what create different rhythms. These are *whole, half, quarter, eighth, and sixteenth* notes.

✓ **Try to tap your foot while you strum**—it is hard at first but keep trying!

✓ **Don't strum all the strings all the time.** Instead, occasionally, use "Bass/Treble" strumming to add interest.

✓ **Listen to and play along** with the audio as much as possible (starting with the slowed-down tracks).

Part II:

Discover The Most Fun, Exciting, and Usable Strumming Patterns Ever

Now that we have covered the basics, the real fun can begin! In this section, you will learn a variety of the most practical and fun strumming patterns out there!

All these patterns will be useful in your playing, each will help you to play lots of great songs and have more fun on guitar. Remember, it is important you have a good grounding of the ideas from *Part 1* before moving forward. If you haven't already, you can download or stream the audio for the book. Just be aware we are now in Part 2, so make sure when you go to the following link you get the audio for Part 2:

rockstarpublishing.co.uk/strum

The Examples for Each Strumming Pattern

There are two audio examples for each strumming pattern. In the audio, the capo is on fret 2 for these examples (as using a capo can make some chords a little easier to play). Feel free to practise them without a capo or place a capo wherever you like.

- **Example #1** is played on a *G Major* chord.
- **Example #2** is played using a popular chord progression.

We will get started with some simple strums and right after those we will quickly build up to the exciting patterns!

The Super Reliable "Starter" Strumming Patterns

We will start with two of the simplest and most reliable strumming patterns out there. These are great starter strumming patterns to begin with.

#1 The "Go-To" Strumming Pattern

This is a super simple strumming pattern that works in lots of situations and is a great strumming pattern to use when you are unsure of what to play.

The "Go-To" Strumming Pattern—Ex. 1

Tracks #1-2   *Capo 2—80 bpm*

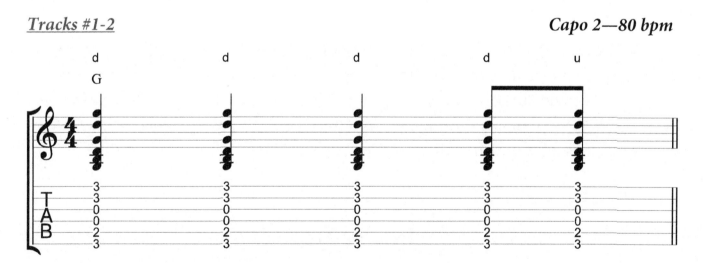

Here is what is happening in the pattern:

- Play four downstrums on each beat.
- Then play an upstrum on the "and" of beat 4.

The "Go-To" Strumming Pattern—Ex. 2

Tracks #3-4   *Capo 2—80 bpm*

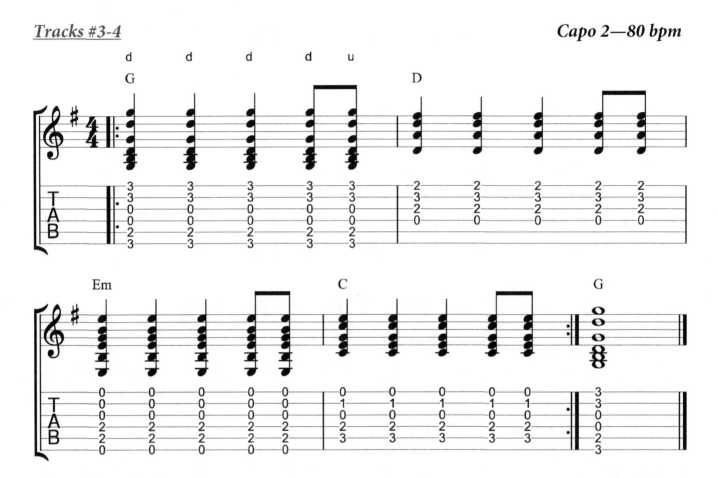

For this example, we are playing the strumming pattern with the popular **G, D, Em, C chord progression**. Above the TAB, in bar 1, you will see the order of down and upstrums (shown by "d" and "u"). Continue this pattern for the rest of the piece. Once again, only bar 1 shows the strumming direction (so as not to clutter things up). Follow these strumming directions for every bar in the example.

Power Tip

Keep a consistent rhythm with the downstrums and remember to try to tap your foot to the beat. This will help you keep a tight groove and can help prevent you speeding up or slowing down.

2—The "Constant Pulse" Strumming Pattern

Next up is the "Constant Pulse" strumming pattern, which is a useful eighth note pattern. Although basic, it can be a little tricky to perfect, so aim to play it with a smooth tone and steady rhythm.

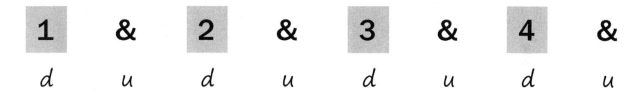

The "Constant Pulse" Strumming Pattern—Ex. 1

Tracks #5-6   *Capo 2—80 bpm*

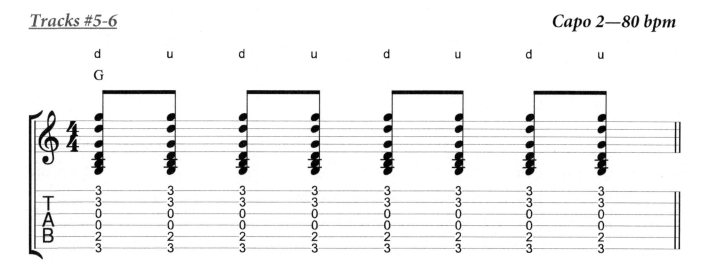

This is what is happening in the pattern:

- Strum down and up in a consistent and steady manner.
- Keep the rhythm and volume even throughout.

Let's start by playing the pattern on a *G Major* chord. Try to get a smooth, clear strum through the strings and revisit the fundamental pointers in *Part 1* if you need to.

39

The "Constant Pulse" Strumming Pattern—Ex. 2

Capo 2—80 bpm

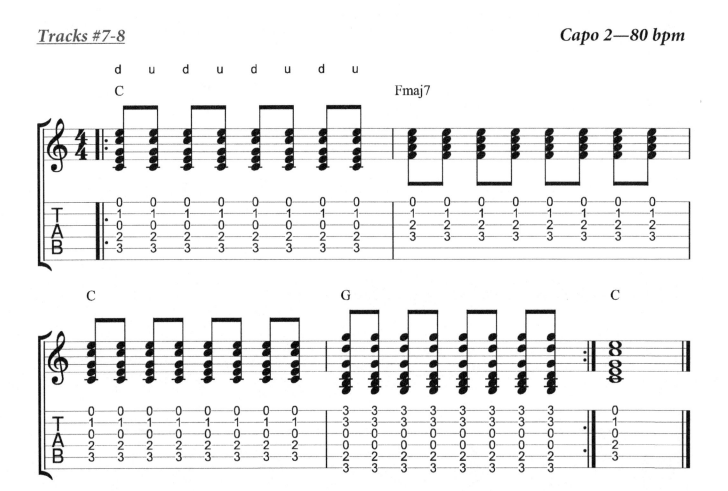

Now we are playing this pattern over a chord progression in the key of *C Major*. To make the chord changes easier, you can "pivot" around your index finger on the 1st fret of the B string as you change from *C Major* to *F Major 7* and back again.

Power Tip

Remember to keep your strumming arm moving up and down in a smooth and even manner—like a pendulum!

The "Big Two" Essential Strumming Patterns

The next two strumming patterns are two of the most useful as they are used a lot. Both patterns utilize fantastic rhythms and are must-learn patterns for all my students.

#3—The "Ultimate" Strumming Pattern

This strumming pattern goes by many names. I once jokingly called it the "Ultimate" strumming pattern to a student, and the name stuck. It is super useful and can be applied to many songs and in many situations.

1	&	2	&	3	&	4	&
d		*d*	*u*		*u*	*d*	*u*

The "Ultimate" Strumming Pattern—Ex. 1

Tracks #9-10   *Capo 2—120 bpm*

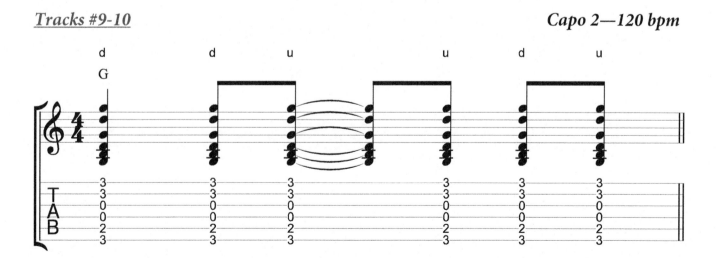

41

DAN THORPE: THE ULTIMATE GUIDE TO STRUMMING

Here are some pointers for this strumming pattern:

- There are two upstrums played one after the other (either side of beat 3)—these are what trip people up the most.
- To get used to them, students often find it useful practising the <u>upstrums on their own</u>, over and over, before attempting the whole bar.
- **Building up the pattern slowly can help you learn it faster**. For example, you could start with **d d u** and then you could add in the next up, so then it would be **d d u u**, and so on.

Listen closely to the rhythm of the pattern, over and over if you need to. Songs that use this strumming pattern include "Brown Eyed Girl" by Van Morrison, and "Hey Ya!" by Outkast. I also use it for acoustic strumming versions of "Sweet Child O' Mine" by Guns N' Roses and "Don't Stop Believing" by Journey.

The "Ultimate" Strumming Pattern—Ex. 2

Tracks #11-12   *Capo 2—120 bpm*

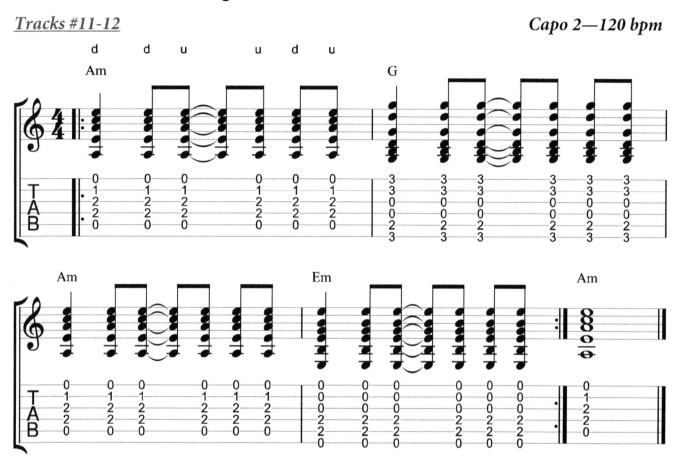

Here we have a simple chord progression in the key of *A minor*. Practise this one steadily, making sure the chords are all crystal clear.

#4—The "Modern" Strumming Pattern

The "Modern" strumming pattern is another essential one. It sounds great, and due to it using a variety of sub-divisions, it has a strong groove. Be patient though, as it can be a tricky one to learn.

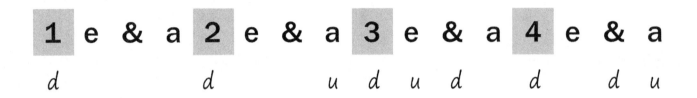

The "Modern" Strumming Pattern—Ex. 1

Tracks #13-14   *Capo 2—80 bpm*

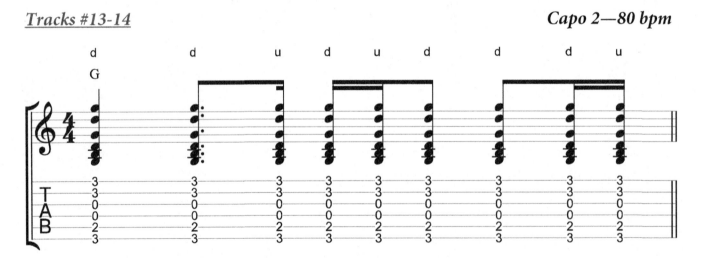

As it is a busy sixteenth note strumming pattern, try to build it up in chunks. This is how I recommend you do so:

- Start with just the initial **d d**
- Then add in the **udud**
- Then, when you can play those two together, add in the **d du** at the end.

Listen to the rhythm of the pattern over and over and keep coming back to it. Students rarely learn this pattern in one sitting.

The "Modern" Strumming Pattern—Ex. 2

Tracks #15-16   *Capo 2—80 bpm*

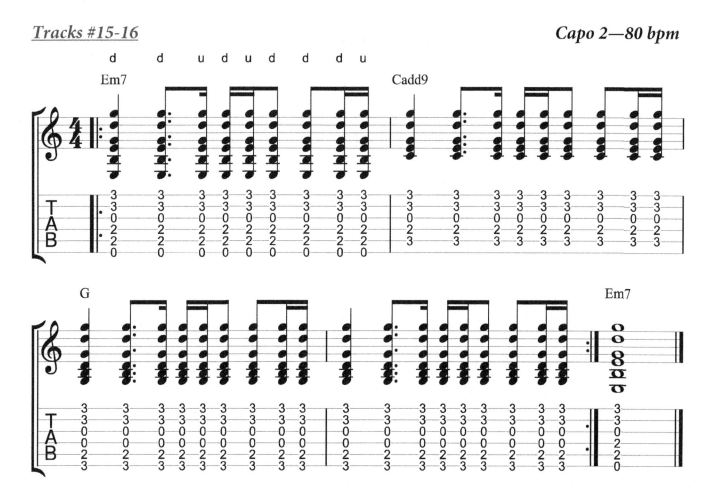

This example uses "chord anchors" which is where you **leave your ring and pinkie** fingers on the 3rd fret of the B and high E strings throughout. There are lots of classic songs that use this pattern or subtle variations of it. These include "Space Oddity" (David Bowie), "Knockin' on Heaven's Door" (Bob Dylan), and "Live Forever" (Oasis).

Contemporary Strumming Patterns to Complete Your Playing

The following two strumming patterns are superb ones to add to your strumming arsenal. Both will give you new and unique grooves and flavours to use.

#5—The "Alternative" Strumming Pattern

The "Alternative" strumming pattern is a contemporary pattern that is played as all **downstrums** but with some important "accents" played on certain beats.

1	&	2	&	3	&	4	&
D	d	d	D	d	d	D	d

The "Alternative" Strumming Pattern—Ex. 1

Tracks #17-18   *Capo 2—120 bpm*

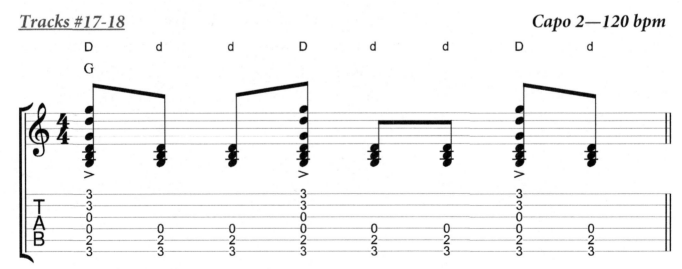

Here are a few tips on playing Ex. 1:

- The accents are all highlighted by the "D" in the diagram above. Play these accented strums a little louder than the rest.
- The rest of the strums are to be played a bit softer.
- For the partial three-string strums, don't try to be too precise. It is okay if you sometimes strum two or four strings instead. The most important thing is you get the groove of the piece correct. (Keep that in mind throughout the book too).

Take your time getting the groove of this pattern sorted. I use this one for songs such as "Best of You" by the Foo Fighters and a strummed version of "Clocks" by Coldplay.

The "Alternative" Strumming Pattern—Ex. 2

Tracks #19-20   *Capo 2—120 bpm*

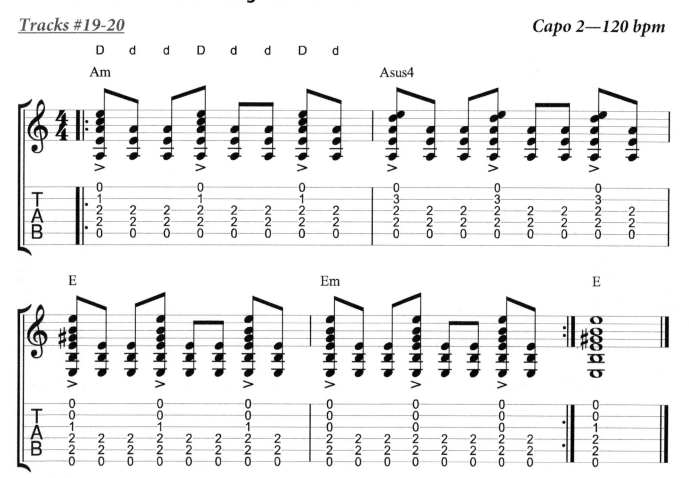

Now we have an interesting example that uses variations of E and A chords. Keep the groove of this piece strong throughout and keep the tempo steady!

#6—The "Piano" Strumming Pattern

This pattern gets its name from the fact it loosely replicates the sound of slower piano songs. Pianists often play ballads in an alternating *loud, soft* manner and this is what we are replicating on the guitar.

The "Piano" Strumming Pattern—Ex. 1

Tracks #21-22   *Capo 2—80 bpm*

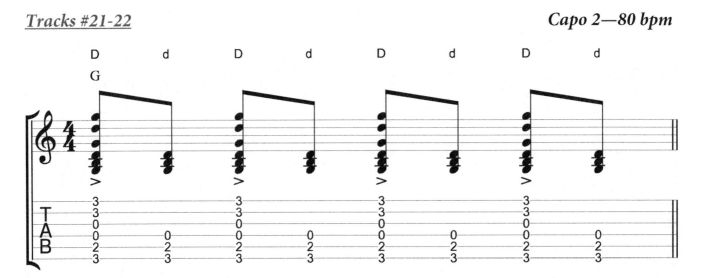

Below are some tips on playing the pattern:

- Use all downstrums for the pattern, ensuring you follow the alternating "loud, soft" feel throughout.
- The Uppercase "D" means loud and lowercase "d" means quiet.
- I tend to strum just the bass strings (low E, A, and D strings) for the softer strums.

You can use this strumming pattern to replicate what the pianists play in songs such as "The Scientist" by Coldplay and the introduction to John Lennon's "Imagine".

The "Piano" Strumming Pattern—Ex. 2

Tracks #23-24   *Capo 2—80 bpm*

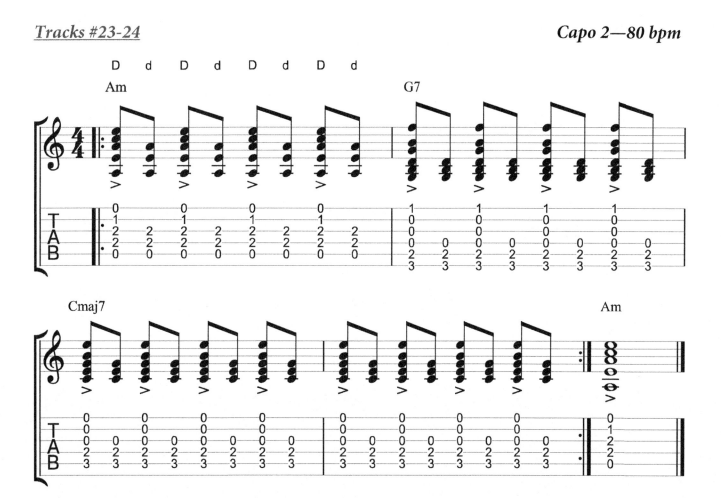

Here we have a pleasant chord progression that brings out the groove of the pattern. Keep the tempo steady and work on each chord on its own if you need to at first.

Power Tip

As always, it will help if you can tap your foot to the beat when playing this pattern. The reason why is that the loud strums will be in time with your foot-tapping and the soft strums will occur when your foot is in the air.

Two-Beat Strumming Patterns for a More Exciting Groove

Now let's look at two-beat strumming patterns. These are patterns that last for, you guessed it, two beats. When playing two-beat strumming patterns, normally you will play the pattern once and then change chords. This means with these strum patterns you will be changing chords more frequently. It is challenging keeping the rhythm going while changing chords often, so keep the tempo steady.

#7—The "Ballad" Strumming Pattern

The "Ballad" strum is a really simple strumming pattern. You will hear it in many slower ballad-type songs, and it generally suits tempos of about 50-80 bpm.

The "Ballad" Strumming Pattern—Ex. 1

Tracks #25-26   *Capo 2—70 bpm*

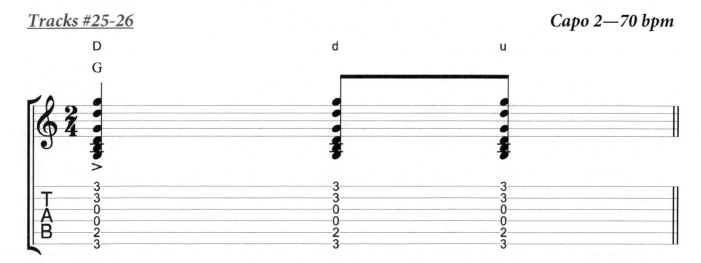

This pattern looks super simple, and it is. Here we have the pattern in a 2/4 time signature (which represents the two beats).

Here are a few pointers on playing this pattern:

- To give the pattern some groove, strum beat 1 a touch harder than the other strums.
- Ensure the rhythm is correct and the tempo is solid, and see if you can tap your foot as you play it.

The "Ballad" Strumming Pattern—Ex. 2

Tracks #27-28   *Capo 2—70 bpm*

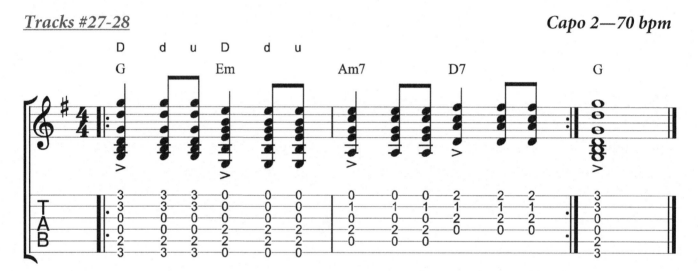

Let's play this pattern with a chord change in each bar. Playing it like this is usually what happens in real songs. Notice how we are playing the pattern twice per bar.

Rhythmically, this is a very simple strumming pattern, but make sure the chords are clear and the upstrums sound good when playing it. The "Ballad" strumming pattern is the one I teach and use for The Beatles classic "Let It Be".

Power Tip

As a reminder from earlier, when strumming upstrums, you only really need to focus on strumming the <u>treble strings</u>. Keep in mind, you do not always need to strum all the strings available to you in a chord!

#8—The "Pop Rock" Strumming Pattern

The "Pop Rock" strumming pattern is another two-beat pattern and a fun, energetic one to add to your repertoire. You will hear this sort of strumming pattern in the 90s hit "Save Tonight" by Eagle Eye Cherry.

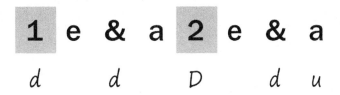

The "Pop Rock" Strumming Pattern—Ex. 1

Tracks #29-30 *Capo 2—80 bpm*

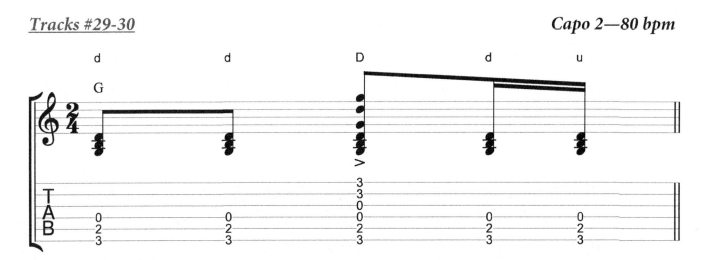

Here are a few tips on playing the pattern:

- **Strongly accent the downstrum on beat 2** (as shown by the "D") while playing the other strums softer.
- **Leave out the tricky upstrum at first** if you need to so you can focus on getting the groove tight.

Take your time getting the groove of this pattern solid. It is all about the strong strums on beat 2. Listen closely and try to tap your foot as you play it.

The "Pop Rock" Strumming Pattern—Ex. 2

Tracks #31-32   *Capo 2—80 bpm*

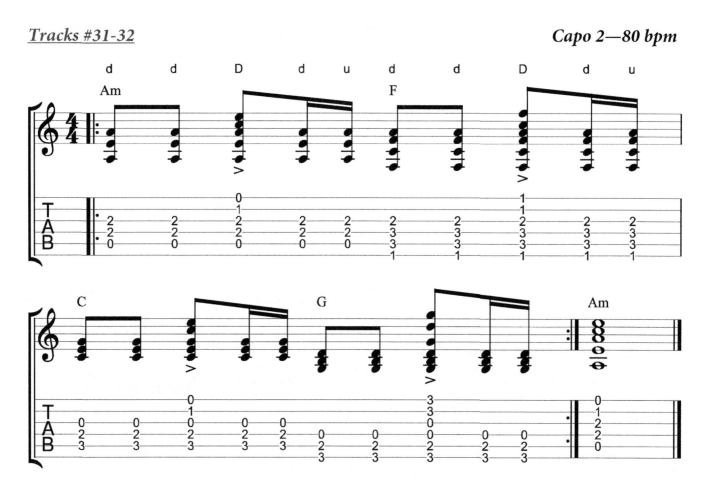

Practise the above piece extra slowly to ensure everything sounds tidy. This pattern and example are not easy, so work on it one chord at a time if you need to. If any chord is tricky, feel free to simplify it or change the chord if you like.

Power Tip

This strumming pattern is all about the groove. Don't try to follow the TAB exactly in terms of which strings are strummed but use it as a template to get the feel of the pattern. The groove is the most important thing here.

3/4 Time Signature Strumming Patterns

Now let's look at strumming patterns that use different time signatures. 3/4 time is not massively popular in modern music but songs such as "Happy Birthday", "Are You Lonesome Tonight", and "The Times They Are A-Changin'" are all in 3/4 time.

#9—The "3/4 Waltz"

The "3/4 Waltz" as I call it is a typical pattern in this time signature that has a bouncy feel to it. This bouncy feel is called "swing" which we will cover more in *Part 3*.

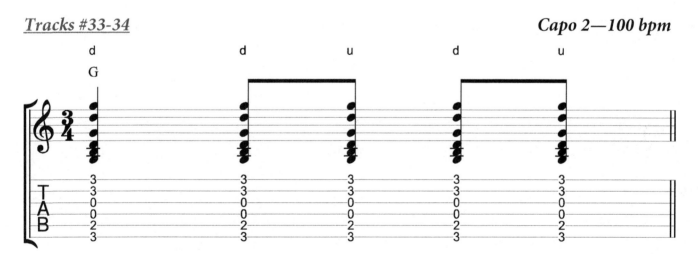

The "3/4 Waltz"—Ex. 1

<u>*Tracks #33-34*</u>   *Capo 2—100 bpm*

Here are a few tips on playing the pattern:

- Try to replicate the bouncy swing feel as heard in the audio.
- Try to tap your foot and count the beats of 1, 2, 3 as you play it.

This is a simple strumming pattern, but remember, to be the most complete strummer you can be, it is important for you to be able to strum in multiple time signatures. Therefore, get it as tidy as you can.

The "3/4 Waltz"—Ex. 2

Tracks #35-36   *Capo 2—100 bpm*

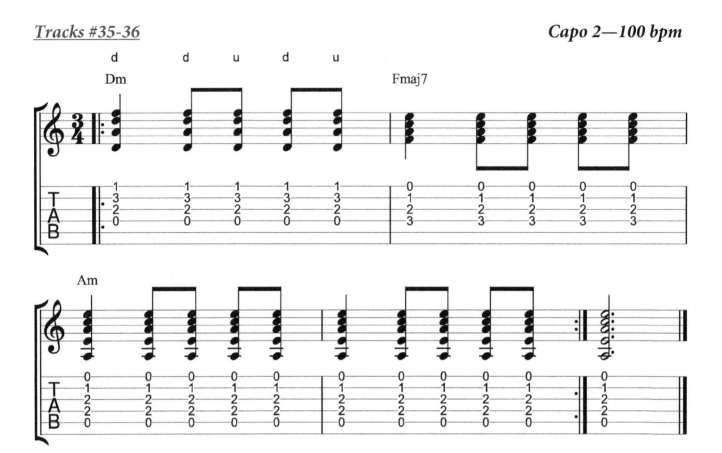

Here we have a simple chord progression based around *D minor, F major 7, and A minor.* Keep the tempo slow and aim to get a smooth and steady strumming sound. If you need to, revisit the tips from *Part 1*. Remember, it takes time to build up good habits.

Power Tip

The "count in" for a piece of music will identify the time signature. As the above examples are in 3/4 time, there will be a 3 beat count-in to signal the piece has a 3/4 time signature.

#10—The "3/4 Flick"

The "3/4 Flick" is a pattern that has a good energy to it. It is a great pattern to use when you want to add more excitement to songs in this time signature.

The "3/4 Flick"—Ex. 1

Tracks #37-38   *Capo 2—100 bpm*

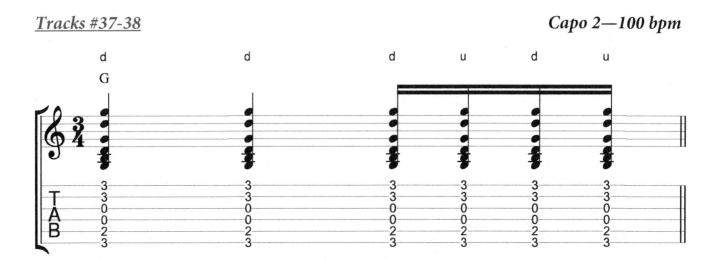

Keep the following in mind as you play the pattern:

- Start with two quarter note downstrums.
- The pattern finishes with four sixteenth notes.

The rhythm in this pattern is a good one to help you practise switching between quarter and sixteenth notes. Keep at it!

The "3/4 Flick"—Ex. 2

Tracks #39-40   *Capo 2—100 bpm*

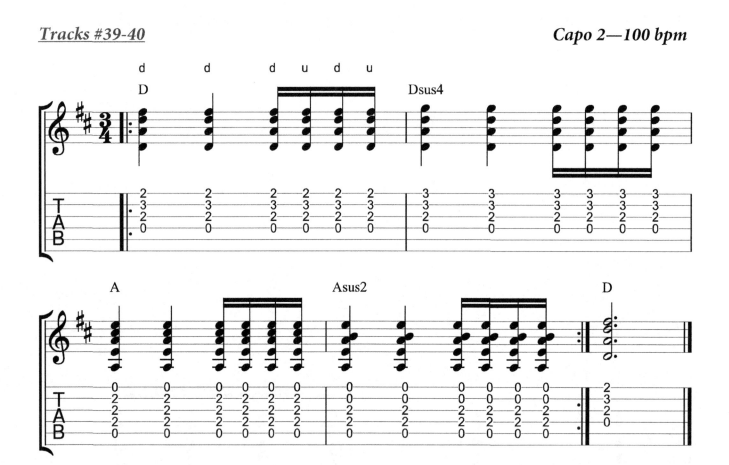

Check that your chords are clear and the changes are smooth throughout this piece. This is a good strumming pattern to use when you want to liven up any song in 3/4 time (e.g., for an intro or instrumental section).

Power Tip

Remember, when mixing up sub-divisions, as we are doing here, it's useful to aim to tap your foot to the beat. If you can, it will help guide you and keep the rhythm solid.

6/8 Time Signature Strumming Patterns

6/8 is a really useful time signature that a good chunk of pop and ballad songs use. Remember, in 6/8 time, there are six beats in a bar. Count them as **1, 2, 3, 4, 5, 6** with the all-important <u>accents on beats 1 and 4</u>.

#11—The "6/8 Groove"

This is a great one to begin with for this time signature, as it is fairly simple and commonly used!

1	**2**	**3**	**4**	**5**	**6**
D	*d*	*d*	*D*	*d*	*d*

The "6/8 Groove"—Ex. 1

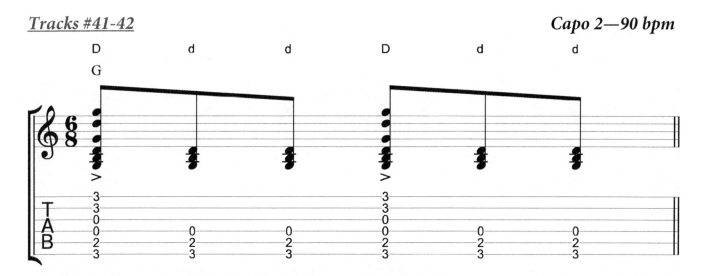

Tracks #41-42   *Capo 2—90 bpm*

This strumming pattern uses all downstrums throughout and here are a few tips on playing it:

- Strum <u>loud, soft, soft, loud, soft, soft</u> (highlighted by the loud strums shown in uppercase in the above diagram).
- Try to tap your foot on beats 1 and 4 (on the louder strums).

The accented beats of 1 and 4 are where you would hear a drummer play his main drum, called the "snare" drum. These beats are important because it is where the audience taps their foot to the beat (if they are in time with the music that is!)

The "6/8 Groove"—Ex. 2

Tracks #43-44   *Capo 2—90 bpm*

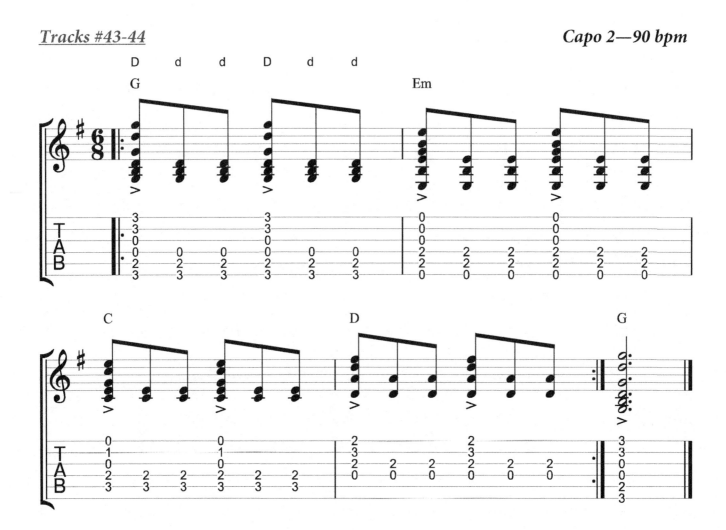

Songs such as "Hallelujah" by Leonard Cohen, "Never Tear Us Apart" by INXS, and "We Are the Champions" by Queen can all be strummed with this pattern. Get it as tight as you can. This example is in the key of *G Major* and uses the *'50s chord progression* (a classic chord progression) which, in this key, means playing the chords of *G Em C D*.

#12—The "Offbeat 6/8"

The "Offbeat 6/8" is a contemporary-sounding strumming pattern with a unique and interesting groove. Listen closely to hear it in action.

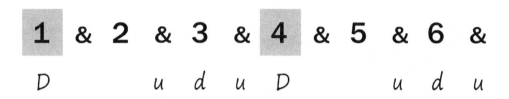

The "Offbeat 6/8"—Ex. 1

Tracks #45-46   ***Capo 2—90 bpm***

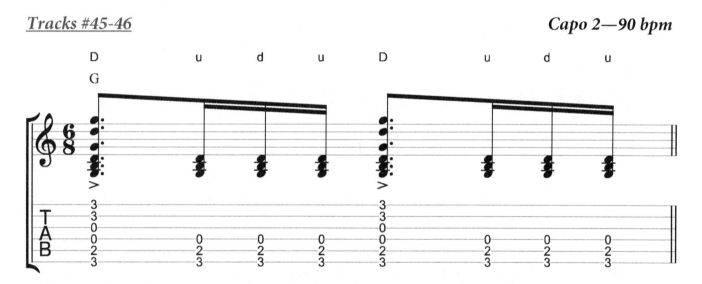

Below are a few tips on playing the pattern:

- The first and second halves of the pattern are the same.
- Accent beats 1 and 4 once again to emphasise the 6/8 pulse.
- Listen closely to the groove as rhythmically this is trickier.

Keep working on this pattern with the *G Major* chord over and over until it sounds like in the recording. To hear a great song that uses this strumming pattern, check out "Elderly Woman Behind the Counter in a Small Town" by Pearl Jam.

The "Offbeat 6/8"—Ex. 2

Tracks #47-48   *Capo 2—90 bpm*

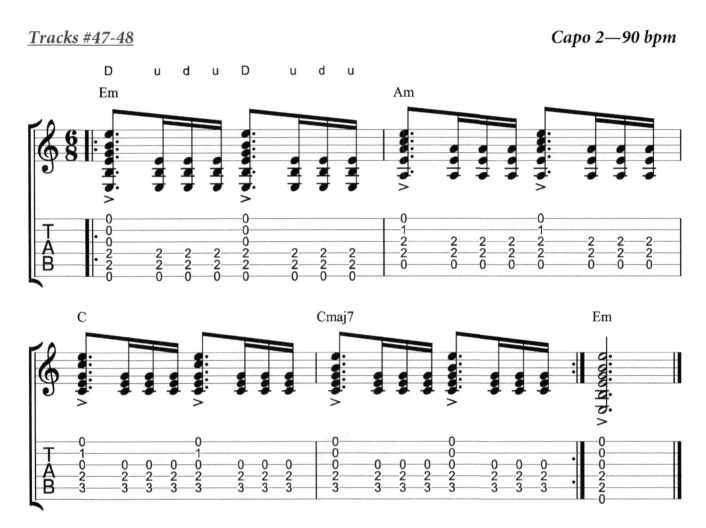

This is a modern-sounding chord progression to practise this pattern with. Work on getting the chord changes smooth before you apply the pattern to the chords.

Power Tip

It is actually quite difficult to count this rhythm, and in my experience, much easier to "feel" the rhythm. Therefore, listen closely to the example above and get playing along!

Strumming Patterns Specific to Certain Genres of Music

In this section, we will look at two very cool strumming patterns used in country and rock (both these patterns are surprisingly flexible). These are all fun and will help add a new string to your guitar playing bow.

#13—The "Country" Strumming Pattern

The "Country" strumming pattern is a very distinct pattern. The rhythm is undoubtedly simple, but the combination of strumming and alternate bass string plucking is what gives it its character.

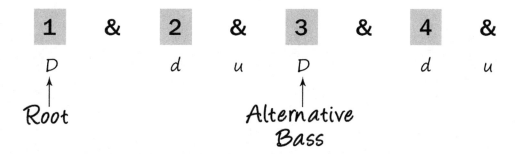

The "Country" Strumming Pattern—Ex. 1

<u>Tracks #49-50</u>   *Capo 2—140 bpm*

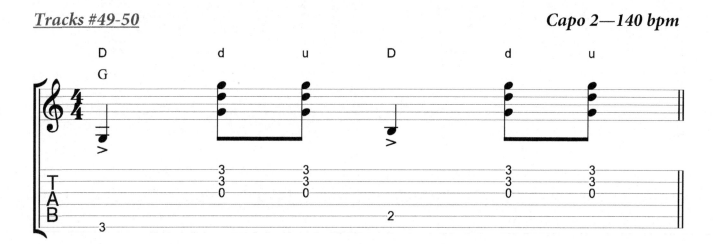

Keep the following in mind as you play the pattern:

- Start with a bass note pluck on the root note.
- Then, strum the chord using down and upstrums as usual.
- Next, pluck an alternative bass note (you will see exactly which string in the TAB).
- Finally, strum down and up again to complete the bar.

With this pattern, it is **important to hear the bass notes clearly,** so pluck them a little harder. When playing the strummed part, we tend to focus more on strumming the treble strings rather than the full chord.

The "Country" Strumming Pattern—Ex. 2

Tracks #51-52   _Capo 2—140 bpm_

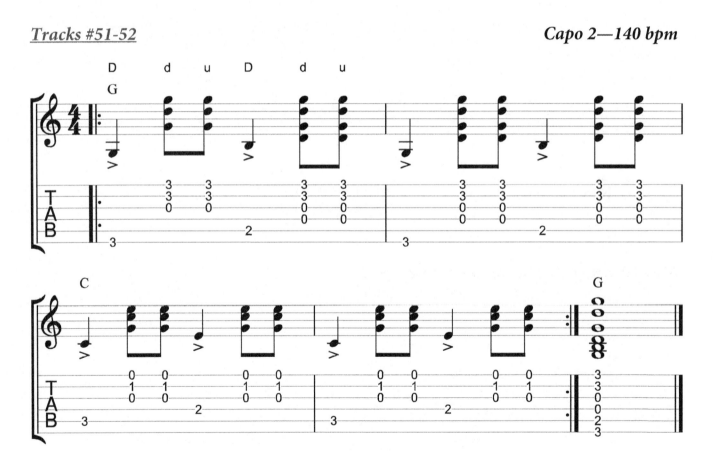

Here we have a typical country chord progression of _G Major_ and _C Major_. You can check out songs such as "A Boy Named Sue" and "Folsom Prison Blues" by Johnny Cash to hear this pattern in use.

#14—The "Power Rock" Strumming Pattern

In many ways, the "Power Rock" strum is one of the easiest patterns of them all. This is because it uses all eighth notes downstrums. It is the speed you play it at that makes this pattern work though!

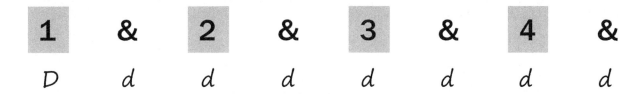

The "Power Rock" Strumming Pattern—Ex. 1

Tracks #53-54   *Capo 2—150 bpm*

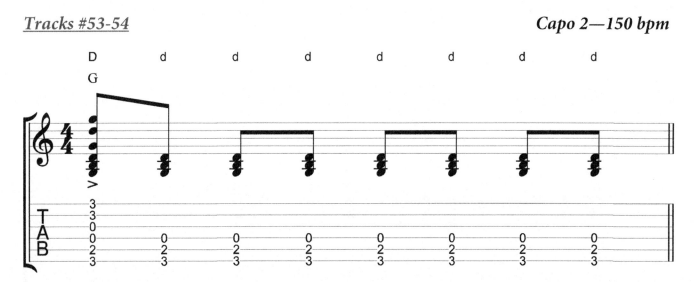

Strum the pattern using all downstrums as this can sound more urgent and aggressive than down and upstrums. This aggression really suits rock!

- Strum loudly throughout and accent beat 1.
- Keep the eighth note rhythm steady throughout.
- If you want to make this pattern sound more "rock", play it on a distorted electric guitar.

Remember, you do not have to strum all the strings in a chord. For patterns like this, you may prefer to focus strumming more on the bass strings as notated. This can make it a fair bit easier to play at faster tempos.

The "Power Rock" Strumming Pattern—Ex. 2

Tracks #55-56   *Capo 2—150 bpm*

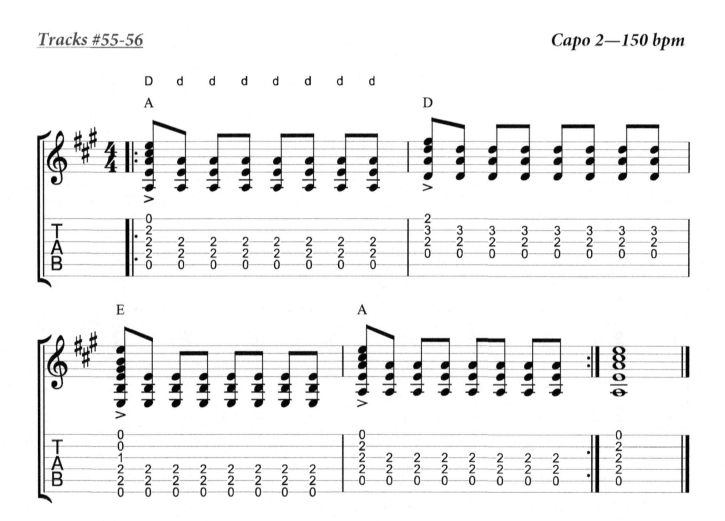

This pattern obviously works well for rock but it can sound great for acoustic strumming too. In fact, I love to use this strumming pattern in some of my acoustic playing—just like in the example above!

The "Fake Drummer's" Strumming Game

Now we have a really powerful game you can play regularly to improve your strumming skills. It is what I call the "Fake Drummer's" Strumming Game.

This is where we play eight of the patterns from Part 2 <u>one after another</u>. Getting good at this game will definitely help you improve your rhythm and strumming skills. Plus, it makes for a fun challenge!

To play the game you can strum some chords but I prefer students to use scratch strums. A "scratch" strum is where you kill off the sound of the strings so they are completely muted. This means you only hear the pure rhythm of the pattern in a percussive, drummer-like way (hence the name "fake drummer"). Scratch strums are great as they take away the distraction of a chord being played, allowing you to focus purely on the rhythm and strumming motion.

The "Scratch" Strum

Achieving a "scratch" strum sound can be tricky at first, so be patient if you have never tried it before. To play a scratch strum, do this:

- Place your fretting hand fingers across **all six strings** using a <u>super-light touch</u>.
- Now strum. If you hear any weird noises, it is likely your fingers are not touching each string OR…
- You may be accidentally applying pressure to the strings somewhere, causing a note to "squeak" out.
- Remember, the strings should

sound <u>dead and percussive here</u>.

Playing the "Fake Drummer's" Strumming Game

On the next page you will see the TAB but before we get there, here are some pointers on playing the game:

- **The "scratch" strums** are shown using a series of "X"s on the TAB. Notice how it is all about the rhythm!

- In the audio, **each pattern is played twice** before moving on to the next one.

- To give a bit of space between each pattern, there is an <u>extra strum on beat 1 of the next bar</u> followed by a pause.

- Accenting the first beat in each pattern can help you hear and feel the start of the pattern better.

- If you struggle with any pattern, <u>go back to the pattern in *Part 2*</u> of the book, and practise it in isolation before coming back to this game.

- **Play the game on your own *without* a click**, and once you can do so, for extra points, practise it *with* a click.

See how far you can get *without* making any rhythmic errors. If you finish the game and can play all of these patterns in a row, perfectly, you win!

Try this fun but challenging game regularly. Practice it slowly, and try to get the patterns as accurate as you can. Getting good at this game will be wonderful for your rhythm skills.

Tracks #57-58

Capo 2—80 bpm

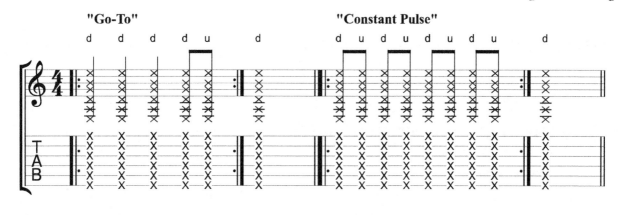

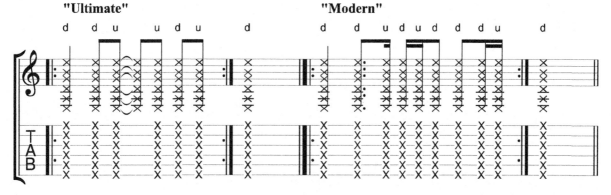

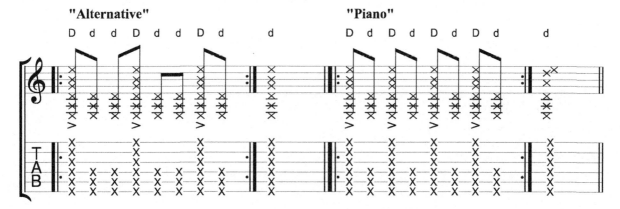

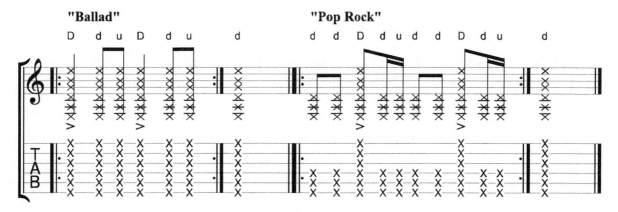

A Fun Strumming Pattern Test

When trying to work out strumming patterns in real songs, at first, it might not always be obvious which pattern is being used.

There is a good chance though that one of the strumming patterns you have learnt in this book will be the right one for the song you want to learn. This little test will help you learn to listen out for and recognise the strumming patterns from the book.

- On the audio tracks below, you will hear a strumming pattern taken from *Part 2* played over an *A Major* chord (with no capo).

- Your challenge is to listen to the audio and write down the names of the strumming pattern being played.

- Listen to the end of the audio track to hear the answers.

Question #1—*Track #59*
Question #2—*Track #60*
Question #3—*Track #61*
Question #4—*Track #62*
Question #5—*Track #63*
Question #6—*Track #64*

Make sure you take the test above and try your best to work out the answers yourself.

For further practice, you can listen to the radio and start listening to a random song. See if you can hear what a suitable strumming pattern would be for that song.

A List of Songs That Use These Strumming Patterns

Here is a list of songs you can use these strumming patterns with. My students and I have created this list over the years and each of the following songs can use the strumming pattern shown in brackets.

The songs on this list are ordered in levels of difficulty but don't take that as gospel. You will likely find some songs easier or harder to play than others. It depends on whether you know the chords, the way you are playing the song, and other factors. You can use the order of this list of songs as a guideline of difficulty though.

Not all of these songs were strummed guitar songs originally. Some were played on the piano and others were fingerpicked rather than strummed. That doesn't matter though, as you can strum pretty much any song out there!

- The Beatles—Let It Be ("Ballad")
- Green Day—Good Riddance (Time of Your Life) ("Ultimate")
- Journey—Don't Stop Believing ("Ultimate")
- David Bowie—Heroes ("Constant Pulse")
- Traditional—Silent Night ("3/4 Waltz")
- Pearl Jam—Elderly Woman Behind the Counter in a Small Town ("Offbeat 6/8")
- Ralph McTell—Streets of London ("Ultimate")
- Oasis—Live Forever ("Modern")
- Van Morrison—Brown Eyed Girl ("Ultimate")
- Bob Dylan—Knockin' On Heaven's Door ("Modern")
- James Blunt—You're Beautiful ("Modern")
- The Calling—Wherever You Will Go ("Ultimate")
- The Smiths—Girlfriend in a Coma ("Ballad")
- INXS—Never Tear Us Apart ("6/8 Groove")
- Sixpence None the Richer—Kiss Me ("Modern")

71

- Prince—Purple Rain ("Modern")
- Coldplay—The Scientist ("Piano")
- John Lennon—Imagine ("Piano")
- The Mavericks—Dance The Night Away ("Constant Pulse")
- Coldplay—Clocks ("Alternative")
- Eagle Eye Cherry—Save Tonight ("Pop Rock")
- Leonard Cohen—Hallelujah ("6/8 Groove")
- Johnny Cash—A Boy Named Sue ("Country")
- David Bowie—Space Oddity ("Modern")
- Eagles—Hotel California ("Modern")
- Echo and the Bunnymen—The Killing Moon ("Ultimate")
- Blur—Country House ("Pop Rock")
- Amy Winehouse—Love Is a Losing Game ("Modern")
- Foo Fighters—Best of You ("Alternative")

Part 2 Summary

That is the end of *Part 2* and here are some tips and key takeaways from this section.

✓ **Do not overload yourself** with learning too many strumming patterns at once.

✓ **Build up a strumming pattern in chunks** if you need to.

✓ **Try to hum** the rhythm of each strumming pattern.

✓ **Get the sound of the pattern <u>stuck in your head</u>**—doing so can help you learn it faster.

✓ **Use one simple chord** to begin with to practise each pattern.

✓ Make sure your chords and changes are as smooth as possible.

✓ **Learn the two super reliable strumming patterns** (the "Go-To" and "Constant Pulse") first, as these are core strumming patterns.

✓ **Master the "big two" strumming patterns** as these are the most useful ever.

✓ **<u>Strumming is all about groove</u>**, so listen, feel, and connect with the rhythm as much as possible.

✓ Try to build up to being able to **tap your foot** to the beat for each strumming pattern you learn.

✓ Get good at playing the **"Fake Drummer's" Strumming Game**.

✓ As a minimum, try to learn <u>5 strumming patterns</u> at least from this section.

✓ **Get good at listening** out for strumming patterns in songs and take the strumming test!

PART III:

LEARN MY MOST EXCITING AND ADVANCED STRUMMING TECHNIQUES

Welcome to Part 3. In this section, you will learn some wonderful techniques that go far beyond the basics of strumming. These are the intermediate strumming techniques my students love the most and now you can learn them too.

Some of the techniques in this section can be a little tricky at first, so do be patient. If you struggle with any of them, do not despair, simply come back and try them again later. They are well worth the effort for what they will do for your playing!

Remember, you can get the audio for the book at the link below (but make sure you get the audio for Part 3 as this is the section we are now in):

rockstarpublishing.co.uk/strum

The Chord Progressions

There are multiple examples for each technique, with the final example using one of the following two chord progressions:

- **Chord Progression #1**—A minor, F Major, C Major, G Major
- **Chord Progression #2**—G Major, D Major, E minor, C Major

Both of these chord progressions are fairly common in songs which makes them good ones for practising the techniques with.

For the following examples, I did NOT use a capo for any of them. Do feel free though to use one when playing them yourself. Just remember to take the capo off when you play along with the audio or you will be in the wrong key!

Simple Tricks to Add More Flavour and Tone to Your Strumming Patterns

Firstly, let's look at three simple techniques that will help you add more excitement to any song and strumming pattern. In this chapter, you will learn how to play strumming variations, play with dynamics, and use "pick strumming".

Strumming Variations

"Strumming variations" are great for keeping songs fresh and when used, can reinvigorate even the most overused pattern. Here we will learn how to play them using the "Ultimate" and "Modern" strumming patterns.

How to Play "Strumming Variations"

To vary a strumming pattern, you essentially do the following:

- Change one or more of the sub-divisions within the pattern. (It can be easier than it sounds).
- Do this while ensuring you keep the core groove of the pattern the same.

Before attempting to vary patterns, make sure that you can confidently play the "stock" version to a good standard. Also, being comfortable with different sub-divisions as mentioned earlier in the book will help too.

Variations of the "Ultimate" Strumming Pattern

Ex. 1A—The "stock" pattern

Tracks #1-2   *No Capo—120 bpm*

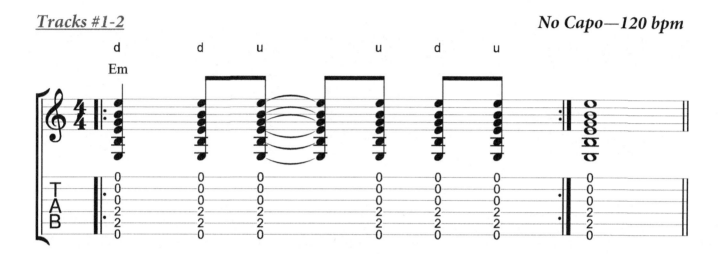

First up, here is a reminder of the "Ultimate" strumming pattern which we learned earlier on in the book.

Make sure you get good at the basic pattern here before trying the following variations. It is never a good idea to try and run before you can walk, so be patient and get rock solid with the "stock" pattern first.

Ex. 1B—Variation 1

Tracks #3-4   ***No Capo—120 bpm***

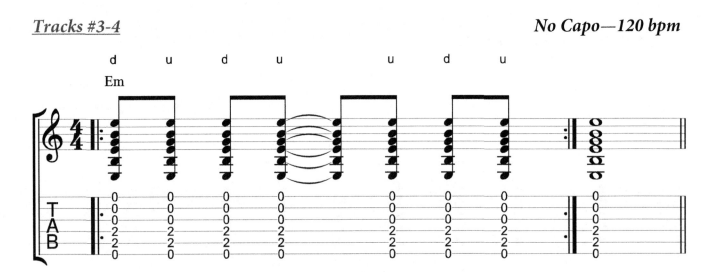

Now, here is the first variation of the pattern. Listen to the audio before trying this example. Can you hear how the groove of the pattern is the same, but there is an extra strum compared to the "stock" version? To play this variation:

- Add in an upstrum on the "and" of beat 1.
- Play the rest of the pattern in exactly the same way as before.
- Keep the overall groove of the pattern the same.

Ex. 1C—Variation 2

Tracks #5-6   *No Capo—120 bpm*

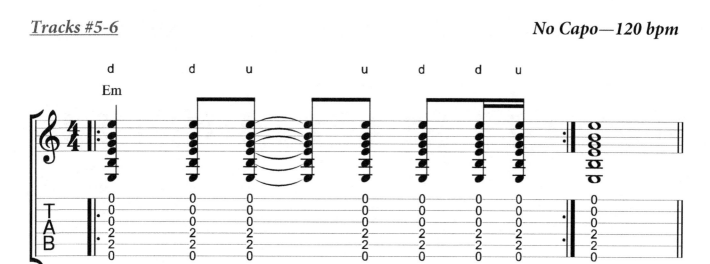

This variation is trickier, so practise it slowly. To play it:

- Remove the last eighth note upstrum.
- Replace it with two sixteenth notes played as a <u>down and upstrum</u>.
- Be patient with this variation and listen to the audio to get it sounding right.

The variation is very subtle but the quicker strums at the end add some nice energy to the pattern. You can use this variation sparingly and when you do, it will sound great.

Ex. 1D—Combining the variations

Tracks #7-8   *No Capo—120 bpm*

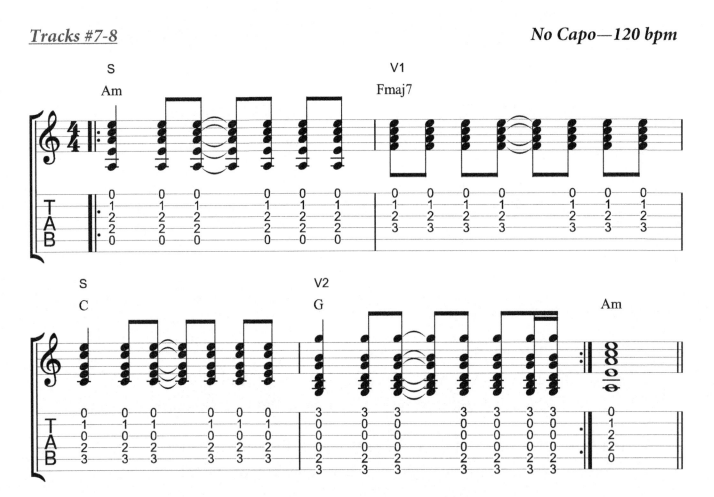

Now, let's combine the "stock" pattern with both of the above variations. We will play them while using *chord progression #1*. Above the notation there are symbols to let you know which variation to use and in which order. This is what they mean:

- "S" = Stock strum
- "V1" = Variation 1
- "V2" = Variation 2

Make sure you can play the stock version and the two variations on their own before putting them together in the above example.

Variations of the "Modern" Strumming Pattern

Ex. 2A—The "stock" pattern

Tracks #9-10   *No Capo—80 bpm*

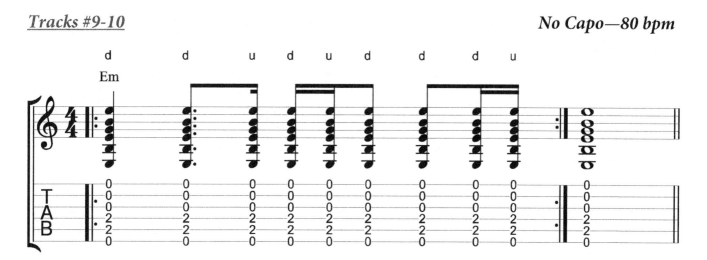

Ex. 2A above shows how to play the "stock" version of the "Modern" strumming pattern.

Ex. 2B—Variation 1

Tracks #11-12   *No Capo—80 bpm*

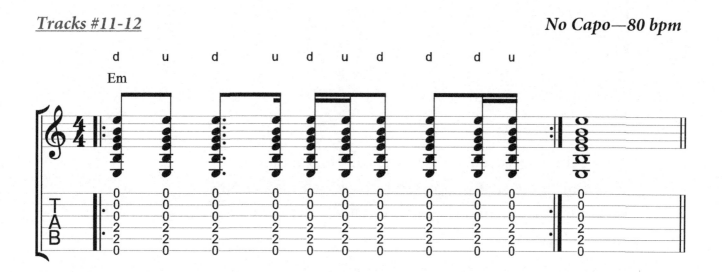

Ex. 2B shows our first variation. Here, there is simply an extra strum right after the first downstrum. To play this:

- Add in an upstrum on the "and" of beat 1.
- Keep the rest of the pattern the same as it was before.

Ex. 2C—Variation 2

Tracks #13-14   *No Capo—80 bpm*

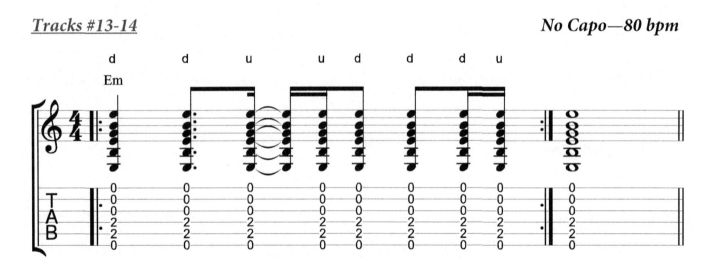

Now, we have a syncopated variation that gives the strumming pattern a subtle but lovely laid-back groove.

- Remove the downstrum on beat 3 to play this variation.
- This means there are <u>two upstrums</u> played one after another.
- This is a tricky variation so practise it slowly and try to keep the groove of the pattern intact.

Ex. 2D—Combining the variations

Tracks #15-16   *No Capo—80 bpm*

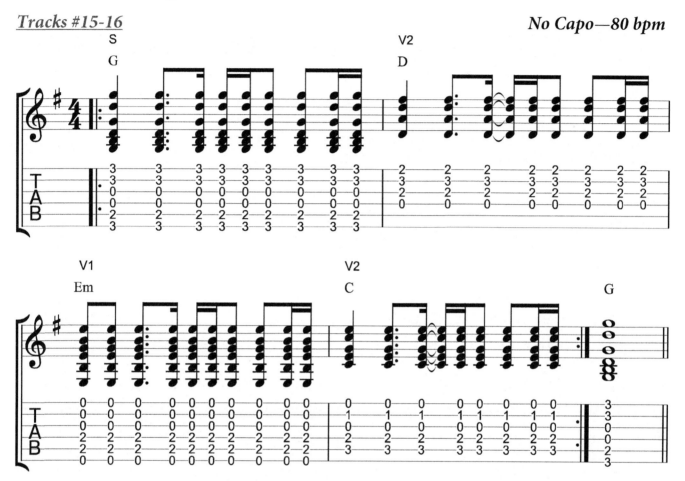

Now we will combine the stock strumming pattern and its two variations. This time we will do so with *chord progression #2*. Again, in the TAB above, there are symbols to let you know which variation to use and when. As a reminder, this is what they mean:

- "S" = Stock strum
- "V1" = Variation 1
- "V2" = Variation 2

Power Tip

See if you can use these variations in songs you know. You can also try creating your own strumming pattern variations. It takes some experimenting to do this, but it gets easier the more you practise, and doing so will help you improve your rhythm skills!

"Dynamics"

The use of "dynamics" simply means how quietly or loudly a piece of music should be played. Varying the dynamics of a piece of music so some parts are louder or softer is one of the simplest ways to add a sense of drama to your playing.

How to Play "Dynamics"

I recommend all guitarists use <u>four dynamic volumes</u>. In music, we generally use Italian words for dynamics and here they are defined for you:

1. *"pp"* = **pianissimo** (very softly)
2. *"mp"* = **mezzo piano** (medium soft)
3. *"mf"* = **mezzo forte** (moderately loud)
4. *"ff"* = **fortissimo** (very loudly!)

Pianissimo and *fortissimo* are the more extreme ends of the dynamic range of the guitar. They are used occasionally for a powerful special effect. *Mezzo piano* and *mezzo forte* are more "standard" volumes that you will use more regularly, so let's start with those.

Practical Dynamics

Ex. 1A

Tracks #17-18   *No Capo—80 bpm*

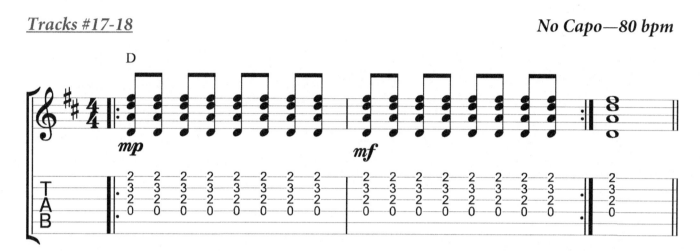

Here, we are using the "Constant Pulse" strumming pattern which, if you remember from earlier, uses all down and upstrums. Let's apply some dynamics to the pattern in the following way:

- **Bar 1—"mezzo piano"** (medium soft)
- **Bar 2—"mezzo forte"** (moderately loud)

The difference in volume between these two is quite subtle, but it is important to be able to switch between them both. Listen to the audio to hear how I interpret these dynamics in my playing.

Ex. 1B

Tracks #19-20   *No Capo—80 bpm*

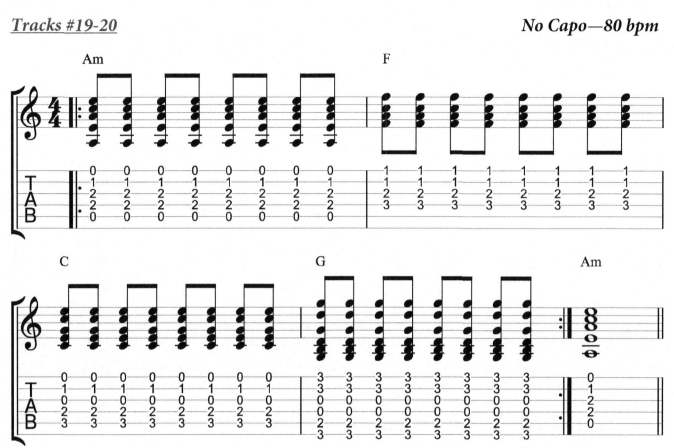

Now, let's take *chord progression #1* and apply both these dynamics to it. The first time play it all as **"mp"** (mezzo piano) and the second time play it **"mf"** (mezzo forte). Listen to the audio to hear that in action.

The Extreme Ends of the Dynamic Range!

Ex. 2A

Tracks #21-22   *No Capo—120 bpm*

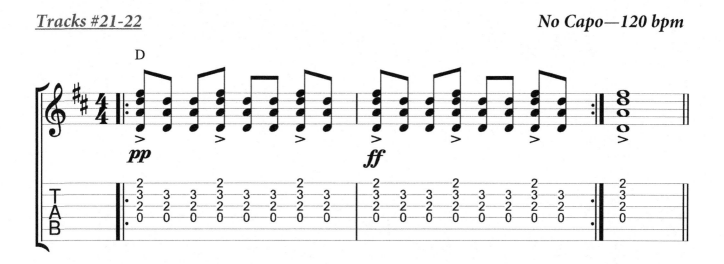

For this example, we will play the "Alternative" strumming pattern (as learnt earlier in the book) using the more extreme range of dynamics. This is how we will use it:

- **Bar 1**—**"pianissimo"** volume (meaning very softly).
- **Bar 2**—**"fortissimo"** volume (meaning very loudly).

Strum as quietly as you can and then as loudly as you can for this example. Although just a practice example, it will help you get used to the more extreme ends of the dynamic range of a guitar which most guitarists rarely ever attempt!

Ex. 2B

Tracks #23-24   _No Capo—120 bpm_

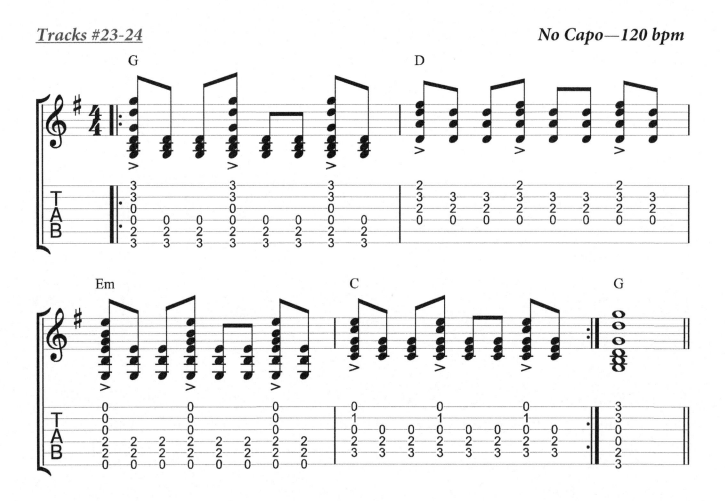

Now, let's try this with _chord progression #2._ Again, play the whole piece using the dynamics as instructed below before switching to the next one.

- **"pp" = pianissimo** (very softly).
- **"ff" = fortissimo** (very loudly!).

You may have never tried strumming your guitar this loudly or this quietly in the past, so it may feel weird at first. Practising this example will help you discover just how much dynamic range your guitar has!

"Pick Strumming"

"Pick strumming" is a technique that many guitarists love the sound of but find difficult to do. Here you will learn how to combine strumming with the melodic plucking of individual strings. Done well it can sound like there are multiple instruments being played!

How to Play "Pick Strumming"

Choose a strumming pattern you are comfortable with and then simply replace a strum (or multiple strums) with a pick of an individual string.

For the first example, we are taking the "Ultimate" strumming pattern and learning to "pick strum" it. Make sure you can play this pattern to a good standard before attempting the examples on the following page.

Adding Melodic Picking to the "Ultimate" Strumming Pattern

Ex. 1A

Tracks #25-26   _No Capo—120 bpm_

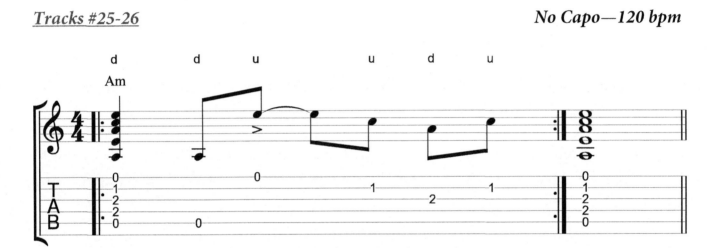

Here, we are taking the "Ultimate" strumming pattern and while keeping the rhythm exactly the same, doing this:

- Strum the first beat as a <u>downstrum</u> as normal.
- Pluck the strings using the down and ups as shown in the TAB.

Remember to keep the rhythm of the strumming pattern in tact. It takes a bit of practise switching between strumming and plucking individual strings, so go slowly at first!

Ex. 1B

Tracks #27-28   *No Capo—120 bpm*

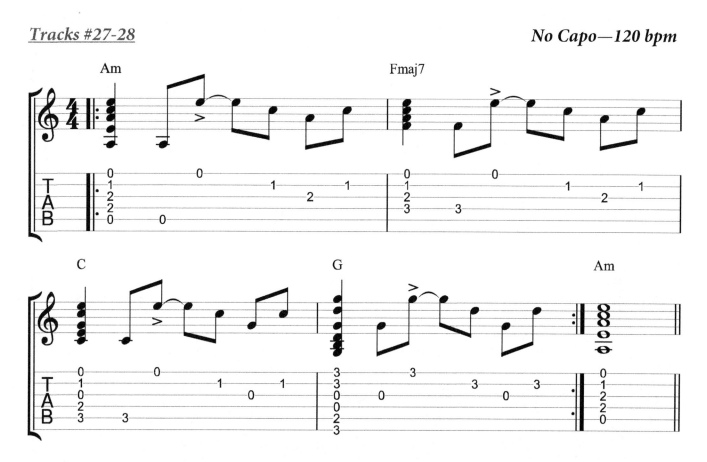

Let's apply the same pattern to *chord progression #1* for a more realistic example. Here we are taking the idea from Ex. 1A but now adapting it to fit the other chords. Practise it slowly.

- (Optional) Leave your index finger on the B string for the *Am, F Major 7, and C* chords—this can help with the chord changes.
- If you lose the groove, go back to strumming the pattern as normal before trying the "pick strumming" example again.

"Pick Strumming" the "Modern" Strumming Pattern

Ex. 2A

Tracks #29-30   *No Capo—80 bpm*

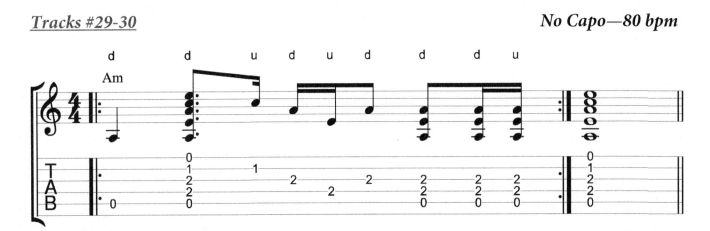

For this example, we are pick strumming the "Modern" strumming pattern.

- Break this example up into <u>small chunks</u>.
- Try to play along with me on the audio to hear how it should sound.
- Don't try to be too precise with the bass note strums at the end.

Try to keep the rhythm of the pattern in tact here. If you strum the odd "wrong" string here and there, don't worry, it will be less noticeable than if you change up the rhythm! Also, make sure you can play the pattern as taught earlier on in the book.

Ex. 2B

Tracks #31-32   *No Capo—80 bpm*

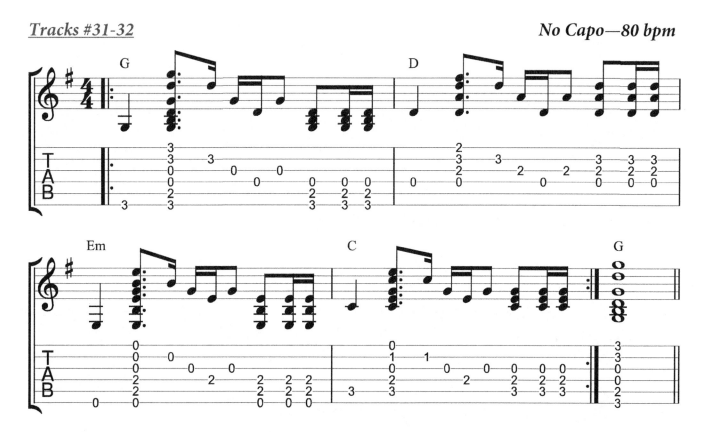

Let's take the exact same idea from Ex. 2A and apply it to *chord progression #2*.

- Get the pattern sounding good on one chord at a time.
- Go steady and build up to this one. It sounds great, but this can be a challenge to play at first. Stick with it though!

Remember, you need a solid foundation of clear chords and smooth changes before you can add the fancy stuff on top.

Power Tip

There is an infinite number of ways you can use "pick strumming". To practise it, try plucking an occasional string instead of strumming it. You can even choose any pattern from the book and try to "pick strum" it. This will be a new skill for many of you though, so keep practising it and keep coming back to it!

3 Ways to Instantly Improve Your Groove

In this chapter, we will develop your sense of "groove". The techniques you will learn include "backbeat percussive strumming", "swing", and using "rests". All three will add energy and excitement to any piece.

Backbeat Percussive Strumming

"Backbeat percussive strumming" is a technique that can give your music a really strong groove. It derives its name from the fact that we are playing a percussive hit on the "backbeat". When played well, this technique can almost sound like you are playing guitar alongside a drummer!

How to Play "Backbeat Percussive Strumming"

This can be an awkward technique to play at first.

- To learn it you will have to stop strumming for a very brief moment to "hit" the strings before you begin strumming again.
- The percussive grooves nearly always land on beats 2 and 4.
- When playing the percussive hit, ensure no strings ring out (or it will sound messy).

The Basic "Backbeat" Percussive Groove

Ex. 1A

Tracks #33-34   *No Capo—110 bpm*

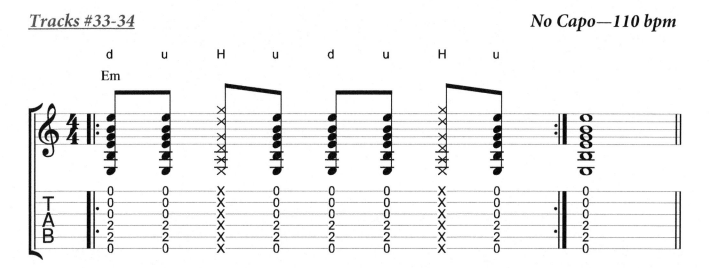

Now then, let's take the "Constant Pulse" strumming pattern from earlier and add a percussive hit to it. These hits are to be played on beats 2 and 4 (shown as "H" in the tab).

- The pattern is played as a **down, up, HIT, up.**
- You then repeat this to complete the bar.

Try to hit the strings with your strumming hand <u>open</u> and not closed. If you keep your strumming hand closed, it will likely be the back of the fingers that make contact with the strings. This can hurt as the treble strings on a guitar are so thin and strong they can feel like cheese wire!

Experiment with opening up the fingers of the strumming hand so that the fleshy side of the fingers and hand make contact with the strings.

Ex. 1B

Tracks #35-36   *No Capo—110 bpm*

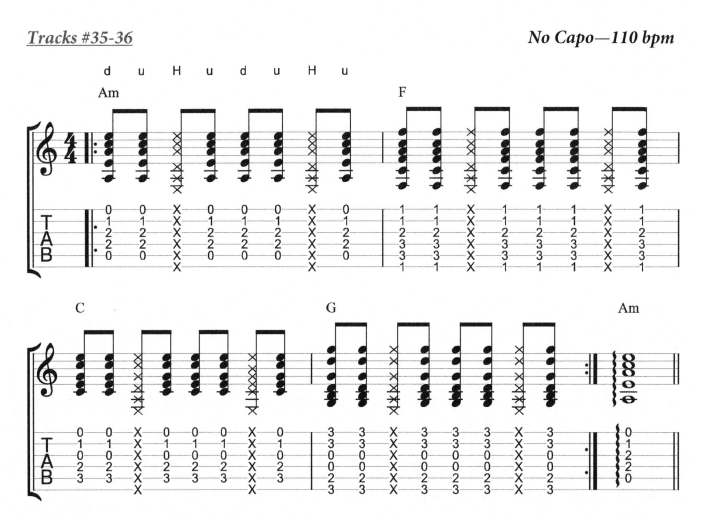

Now, let's take the same rhythm pattern and apply it to *chord progression #1*. One thing you should note is this:

- The percussive hits are followed by upstrums.
- Therefore, try to <u>prepare your strumming hand so it is ready to strum upwards</u> right after the hit.

If the big, full barre chord version of F Major is a challenge, feel free to use a stripped-back easier version of it (like the one used on page 86). Alternatively, I have a course that goes deeply into barre chord playing technique. (Go to **rockstarpublishing.co.uk/barres** for more information).

"Backbeat percussive strumming" is an awkward skill to master at first and is unlike many other techniques. Therefore, be patient with it.

A Stylish Sounding Percussive Backbeat

Ex. 2A

Tracks #37-38   *No Capo—120 bpm*

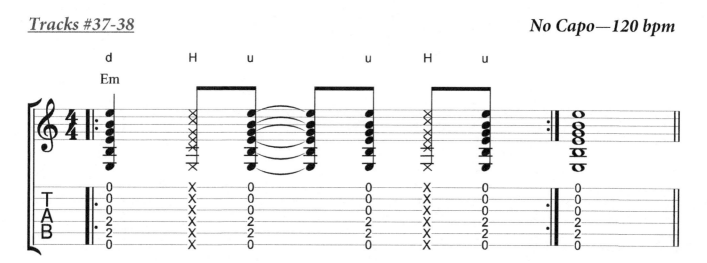

Now then, let's take the "Ultimate" strumming pattern and apply percussive hits to it.

- The pattern is played this way—down, HIT, up, up, HIT, up.
- Once again, the percussive hits are on the backbeat of beats 2 and 4.

Remember, you need to be able to play the core strumming pattern from earlier on in the book before attempting this example. Adding in the hits to the pattern like this can make it sound even better!

Ex. 2B

Tracks #39-40   *No Capo—120 bpm*

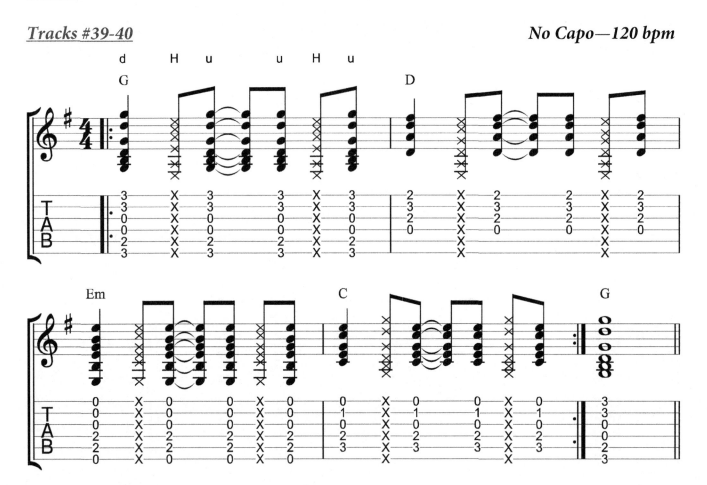

Finally, let's apply the same idea from the previous example, but now with *chord progression #2*.

- Ensure each chord is clear and each change is smooth.
- Listen closely to the audio so you can clearly hear the rhythm of the piece.

Remember, if you like, you can use a capo when practising any of these examples if that helps.

Power Tip

Don't rush! This will be a brand-new technique for many of you, so take your time and practise it very slowly, ensuring each strum is clear and each hit has a tight percussive sound.

Swing

"Swing" is a simple way of adding life and soul to a strumming pattern. I like to think of swing as "bounce" and it works better at slower tempos (faster tempos tend to nullify the sound of swing a bit).

How to Play "Swing"

For a bit of background, there are two main "feels" in music which are:

- **Straight feel**—the standard feel which is quite "mechanical".
- **Swing feel**—a more distinctive, "bouncy" feel.

Swing is shown in music notation by this symbol to the right.

Below is a visual guide of the "Constant Pulse" strumming pattern used to highlight straight and swing feels. Firstly, you will see it as a straight feel (as we learned earlier).

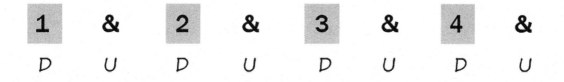

Now you will see the strumming pattern notated with the bouncy "swing" feel.

In the second diagram showing "swing", each upstrum is shifted to the right slightly to show it should be <u>delayed</u>. That is a technical view of what is happening with swing, but for most guitarists, it is better to hear swing in action. Let's do that now…

A Simple Way to Learn to "Swing"

Ex. 1A

Tracks #41-42   *No Capo—80 bpm*

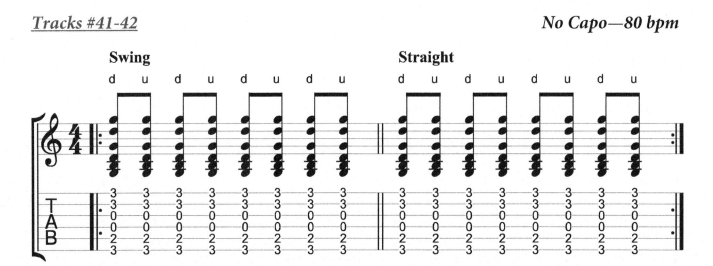

Let's use the "Constant Pulse" strumming pattern for this example. This is how we do so:

- **Bar 1**—play the pattern with "swing".
- **Bar 2**—switch back to a mechanical "straight" feel.
- Playing along with the audio can really help you get the feel for both of the above.

In a real piece of music, you wouldn't usually alternate between straight and swing in the same piece of music like this. This example is simply there to help you clearly hear the differences between the two feels and get you practising swing feel.

Ex. 1B

Tracks #43-44   *No Capo—80 bpm*

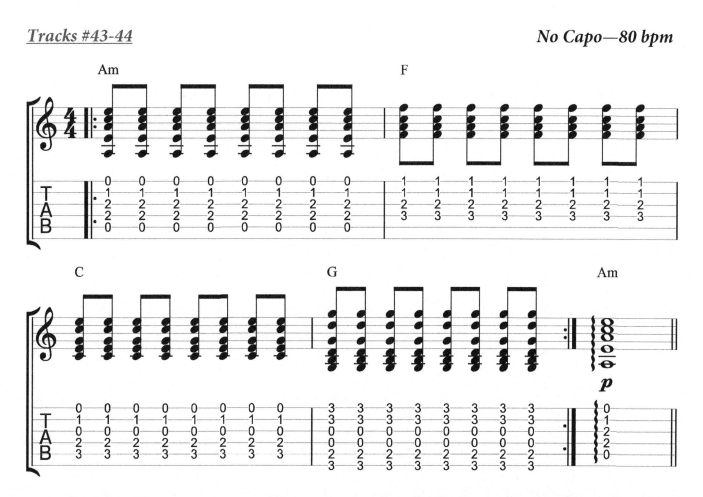

Let's play *chord progression #1* once again with both feels. Here is how it will sound:

- First time—play the piece with a <u>"swing" feel</u>.
- Second time—play it with a <u>"straight" feel</u>.

When playing a piece, there are no rules for which feel you should use—only what sounds best for the situation. For fun, try adding swing to a song you know!

Swinging the "Ultimate" Strumming Pattern

Ex. 2A

Tracks #45-46   *No Capo—120 bpm*

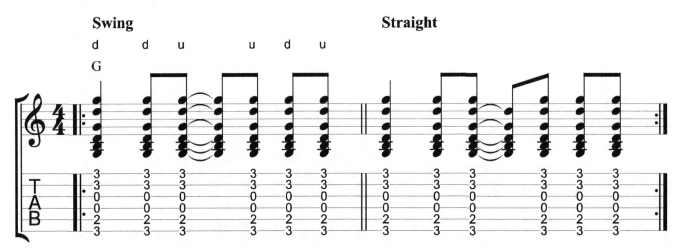

The next strumming pattern we will swing is the "Ultimate" strumming pattern. Here's how:

- Bar 1—play it with "swing".
- Bar 2—play it with a "straight" feel.

You may notice there are fewer upstrums in this pattern. This means this example of "swing" is more subtle. Listen closely though and you will hear the bounciness of the swing there.

Ex. 2B

Tracks #47-48   *No Capo—100 bpm*

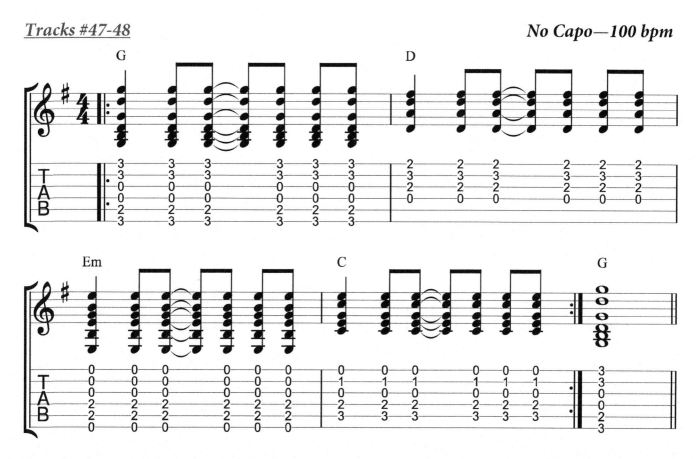

Our final swing example applies the same idea as before, but now using *chord progression #2*, like this:

- First time—play the piece with a "swing" feel.
- Second time—play it with a "straight" feel.

If you struggle to get the feel correct, keep playing along with the audio. It can really help!

Power Tip

When it comes to swing, you can think logically about it and try to delay your upstrum a touch. Most guitarists find it more useful to mimic the "bouncy" sound of swing by listening to it in action though.

Using "Rests" to Add a Powerful Energy to a Piece

Rests, often called "staccato" (an Italian musical term meaning detached), are simply moments of silence. Don't dismiss them though, they can add a lot of energy to a piece of music and can help you take a tired, old strumming pattern and instantly give it a new lease of life!

How to Play "Rests"

The easiest way to add rests to your music is to use your strumming hand to stop the sound of the strings.

- To do this, place the <u>strumming hand on the strings</u> in the area you strum.
- Ensure you silence all of the strings and don't let any string noise ring out.

Alternatively, you can use your fretting hand to kill the strings by resting a finger(s) across the strings. For most people though, in this context, the technique of muting strings is easier to do with the strumming hand.

Staccato Downstrums

Ex. 1A

Tracks #49-50   *No Capo—100 bpm*

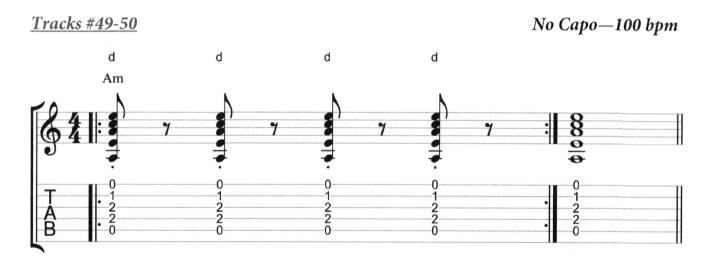

Our first example of the technique is a practice exercise played on an *A minor* chord.

- Here, we are playing four choppy downstrums.
- To begin with, strum a <u>downstrum as usual</u>.
- Then stop the sound with the strumming hand to create the first <u>"rest"</u>.
- Repeat this process for a total of four "choppy" staccato strums.

Practise this slowly at first and ensure there is complete silence between each strum. Listen closely to the exact rhythm in the audio before attempting it.

Ex. 1B

Tracks #51-52   *No Capo—100 bpm*

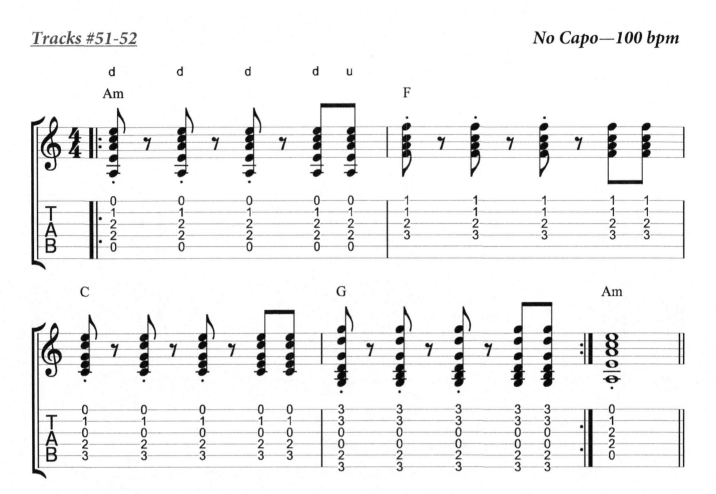

This example of using "rests" is one of my favourites. You will hear this type of technique in energetic rock and pop songs. The first bar shows the order of down and upstrums but carry the same pattern on throughout the piece.

- There are <u>three "choppy" strums in each bar</u>.
- The end of the bar features a normal down and upstrum (without rests).

Listen to the audio closely, and once again, work on one chord at a time before putting the chord progression together as a whole.

How to Add Rests to Supercharge the Most Common Strumming Pattern Ever!

Ex. 2A

<u>*Tracks #53-54*</u>   *No Capo—120 bpm*

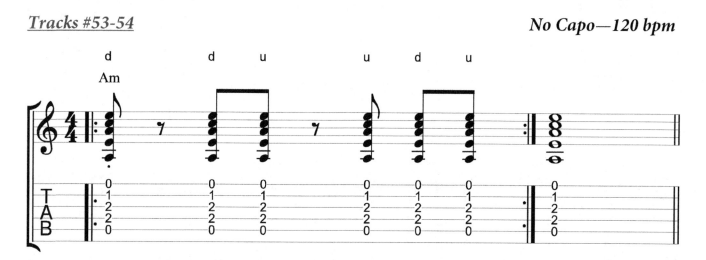

Now let's take the "Ultimate" strumming pattern and add rests to it. This will give the pattern more energy but do revisit the strumming pattern from earlier on in the book if you need to.

- There are **two rests** added to the "Ultimate" strumming pattern here.
- The first rest is directly after the **first <u>downstrum</u>**.
- The second rest is directly after the **first <u>upstrum</u>**.

Take your time getting this rhythm correct, as it can be awkward at first. Listen to how adding a rest to this strumming pattern creates a totally different groove and feel to it compared to when strummed without them!

Ex. 2B

Tracks #55-56   *No Capo—120 bpm*

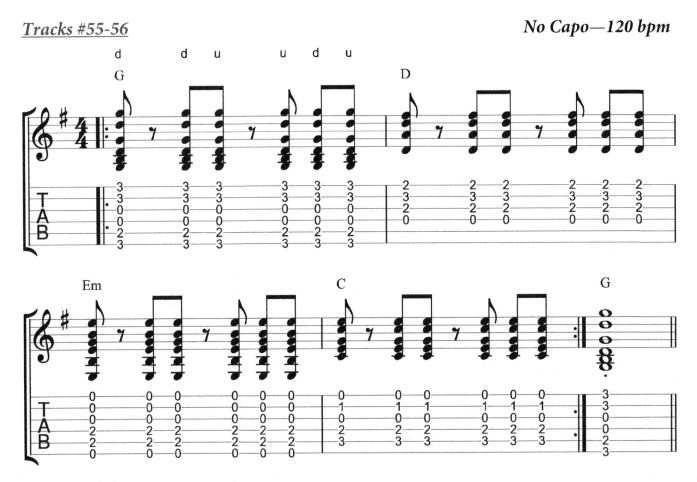

Finally, let's take the above version of the "Ultimate" strumming pattern, and apply it to *chord progression #2.*

It can be hard coordinating your hands to strum, play the rests, AND change chords. Therefore, take your time getting this technique sorted and don't rush!

Power Tip

Remember, a rest should mean <u>complete silence</u>. If there is not complete silence rests will lose their power and the music may just sound messy. Therefore, go very slowly with these examples and work on one chord at a time until it all sounds great!

The Stylish and Sophisticated Techniques Used by the Pros

Now then, let's learn some of the most stylish and sophisticated techniques you no doubt have heard many pros use on a regular basis. These include embellishing chords, playing bass riffs, and taking inspiration from drummers to play "strumming fills". Let's start with embellishments…

"Exciting Embellishments"

An embellishment is simply a way to add some melody to a chord. To embellish a strumming pattern you simply remove, add, or move fingers to the chord while strumming it. When played well it can sound like you are combining rhythm and lead!

How to Play "Embellishments"

There are three ways to embellish a chord. These are:

- Remove a finger from a chord.
- Add an unused finger to a chord.
- Move a finger to a different string or fret.

Whenever you remove, add, or move a finger, it is usually a good idea (if possible) to try to keep the other fingers on the chord (this will let more notes ring out).

Embellishing One Bar at a Time

Ex. 1A

Tracks #57-58 *No Capo—120 bpm*

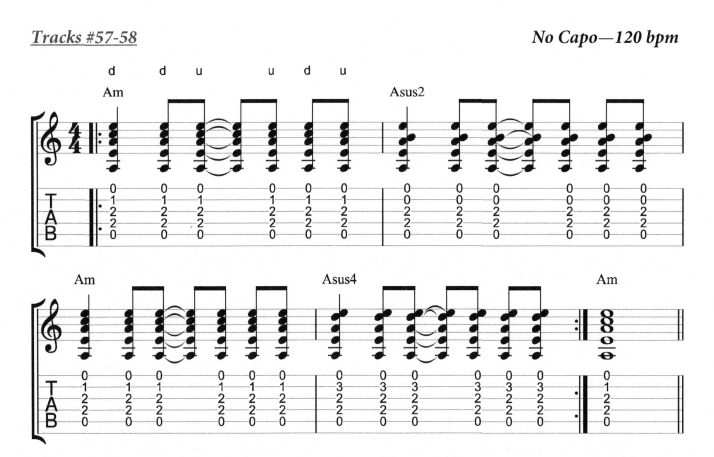

The first example uses an *A minor* chord and the "Ultimate" strumming pattern. Below is what is happening in each bar:

- Notice how in each bar the note on the B string changes.
- For example, in bar 1, the note is on the 1st string, then bar 2 it is open and so on.

When adding and removing fingers from the chord, the chord name changes slightly. The exact name of the chord isn't important here though—it is the embellishment that counts. (Although it is good to eventually learn the names of these chord variations).

Ex. 1B

Tracks #59-60   *No Capo—120 bpm*

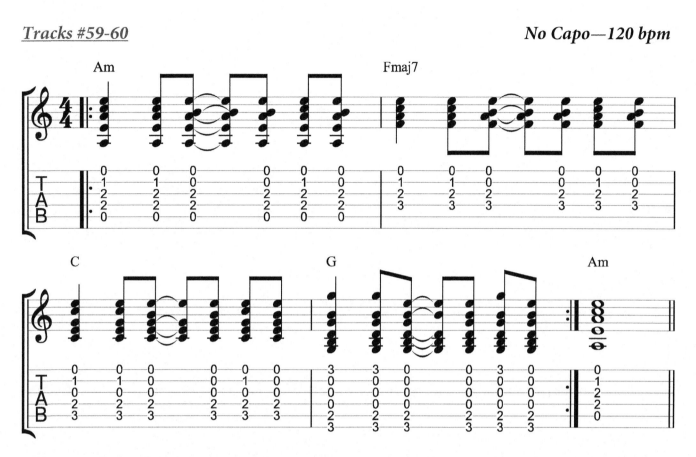

Now, let's develop this idea further with *chord progression #1*. Here we are embellishing the chord <u>during</u> the bar.

- In bars 1-3, your index finger will be lifted off and on the B string multiple times during the bar. (In bar 4, whichever finger is on the high E string will be lifted off and on).
- This is a tricky little piece, so just like everything else, practise it very slowly at first. The speed will come as your ability (and confidence in playing the piece) increases.
- View the TAB closely to see what is happening. Go slowly at first as coordinating both hands like this can be difficult.

The good thing here is that bars 1-4 all embellish at the <u>same point</u> in the bar.

Embellishing the "Modern" Strumming Pattern

Ex. 2A

Tracks #61-62   *No Capo—80 bpm*

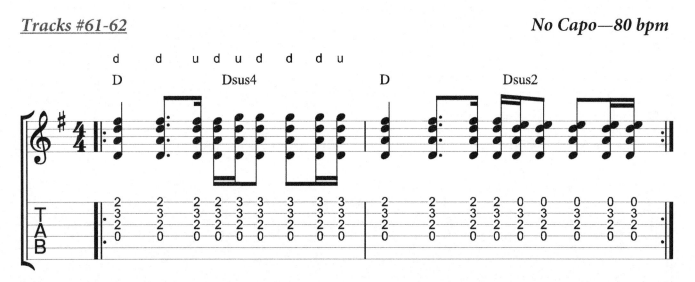

Now let's embellish the "Modern" strumming pattern on a *D Major* chord. This is what is happening here:

- In bar 1, we add the pinkie on the high E string at fret 3 (at about the halfway point).
- Bar 2 starts off with a normal *D Major* chord again but then you remove a finger to create an open high E string (again at the halfway point).

Be as precise as possible when learning techniques like this and if it helps, remember, you can use a capo to potentially make things easier for the fretting hand.

Ex. 2B

Tracks #63-64   *No Capo—80 bpm*

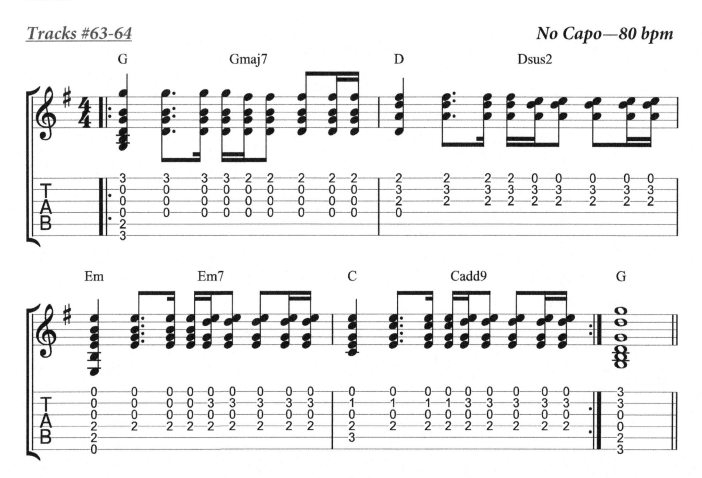

Now, we are taking the previous example and applying it to *chord progression #2.*

- Be careful to stay on your fingertips when adding and removing fingers within a chord. If not, the chord can get messy quickly.
- When using this technique, it is a good idea to focus your strumming a little more on the treble strings. This will help to ensure the melody gets heard.

As always, work on one chord at a time before putting it all together.

Power Tip

An important point—if you can't hear the melody being played, there is no point in doing it. Always focus on making sure the string being embellished can be clearly heard!

Bass Riffs

A really fun way of adding interest to your strumming is to use the occasional "bass riff". These sound great, are melodic, and can be used to link from one chord to another nice and smoothly.

How to Play "Bass Riffs"

There are no rules on how to play bass riffs, but it is a good idea to use **scale notes** from the key you are in. For example, if you are playing in the key of *G Major,* use the G Major scale. Some people prefer to use their ear to help them decide what sounds good. I like to use a combination of both.

Although certainly not always possible, try to leave as many fingers in the chord fretted for as long as possible. This will allow the chord tones to ring out and keep the music sounding fuller.

A Stylish and Groovy Bass Riff!

Ex. 1A

Tracks #65-66   *No Capo—70 bpm*

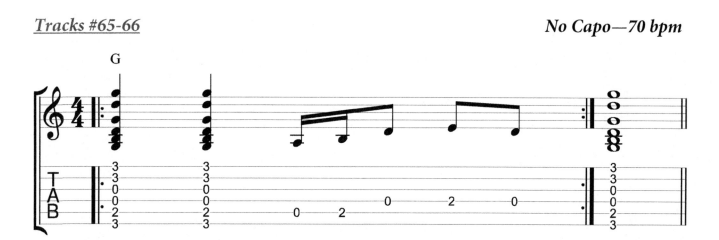

In the first example, we will use a bass riff based around the chord of *G Major*.

- Play two downstrums to begin with.
- Next, play the five notes as shown in the TAB above.

In terms of the bass riff, you can pluck using all downs, a combination of downs and ups, or you can even use hammer-ons/pull-offs for the notes in this example if you prefer. Get the groove of the bass riff nice and tight here.

Ex. 1B

Tracks #67-68   *No Capo—70 bpm*

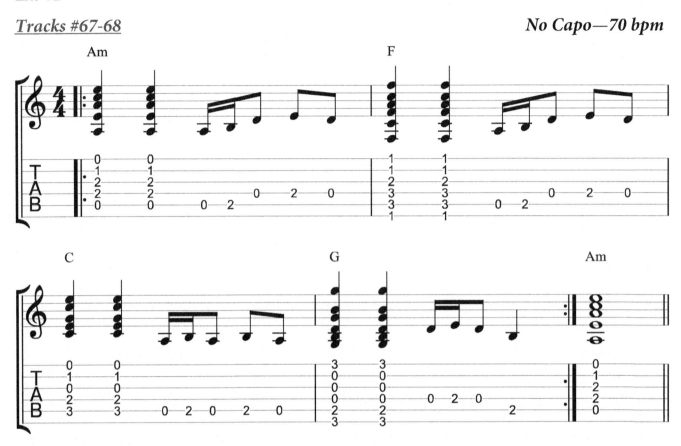

Now we are taking the same concept and rhythm from the previous example and playing it over *chord progression #1*.

- You will probably need to <u>remove some fingers from each chord</u> to play the bass notes at various points.
- Pluck the bass riff notes a little harder to make them stand out.

Work on each bar in isolation and notice how the rhythm is the same for each bar—it is <u>just the notes and chords that change</u>.

A Subtle "Leading" Bass Run

Ex. 2A

Tracks #69-70   *No Capo—70 bpm*

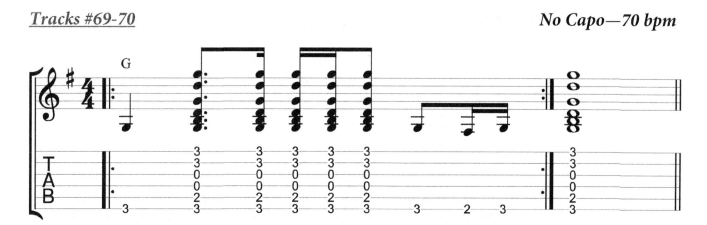

This example is based on the rhythm of the "Modern" strumming pattern. You can break it up into the following three parts:

1. Start with a simple bass note pluck followed by a full downstrum.
2. Next, strum the middle section of the bar using an up, down, up, down motion.
3. Finally, there is the simple three-note bass riff at the end.

Remember, it is important to keep the rhythm of the "Modern" strumming pattern intact for this example.

Ex. 2B

Tracks #71-72   *No Capo—70 bpm*

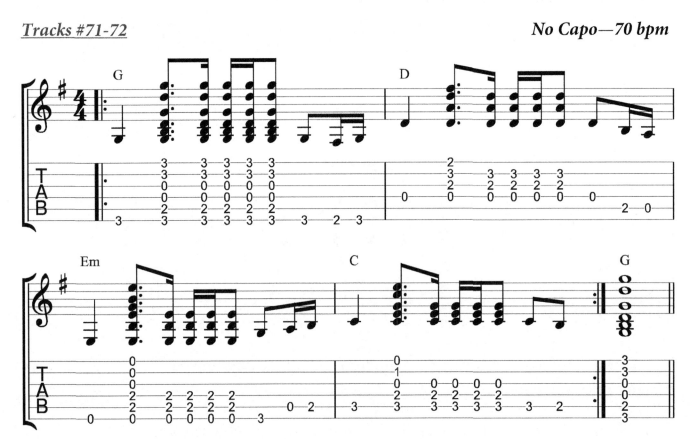

Now, we will develop the previous idea. This one shows you don't need complex bass riffs to make interesting music!

- Each bass run is slightly different here so work on one bar at a time.
- All four bars are good examples of how to use bass riffs to melodically <u>link other chords</u>.

Don't be too strict on which strings you strum in the strumming pattern, but ensure the rhythm and bass riffs are correct—they are both the priority here.

Power Tip

Hit the bass notes a little harder to highlight them and make them noticeable for the listener. If you don't, these notes will get buried underneath the chord, and this can sound a little odd. Get it right, and it sounds great!

Strumming Fills

"Strumming fills" are a way of adding exciting transitions from one section of a song to another. The technique is a simple one based on what drummers do as they switch from a standard drum beat to a drum "fill". That process is what we are replicating here on guitar.

How to Play "Strumming Fills"

Strumming fills create and build up tension, energy, and excitement in a piece as it moves towards a new section, such as when transitioning from a verse to a chorus. There are no set ways of playing drum fills but listen to drummers and try to mimic the timing and feel of what they do. Here are a few good examples of strum fills to get you started:

The "Build Up" Strumming Fill

Ex. 1A

Tracks #73-74

No Capo—100 bpm

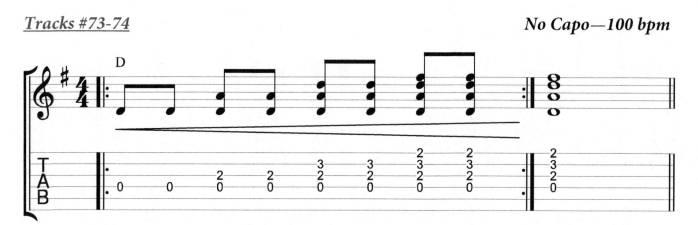

Our first example is a classic based on a very popular drum fill. It makes for a great transition as a song moves into new sections.

- Use all downstrums throughout.
- To create the groove, start off quietly and <u>gradually build up the volume</u>.
- As you get louder, <u>strum more strings</u> to build up the sound even more.

119

The strings being strummed in the TAB are a guide and don't have to be followed exactly. In the audio, we are repeating this bar just to get you playing it and practising it more. In practice, you would only play this sort of fill once before the next section of the song comes in.

Ex. 1B

Tracks #75-76   *No Capo—120 bpm*

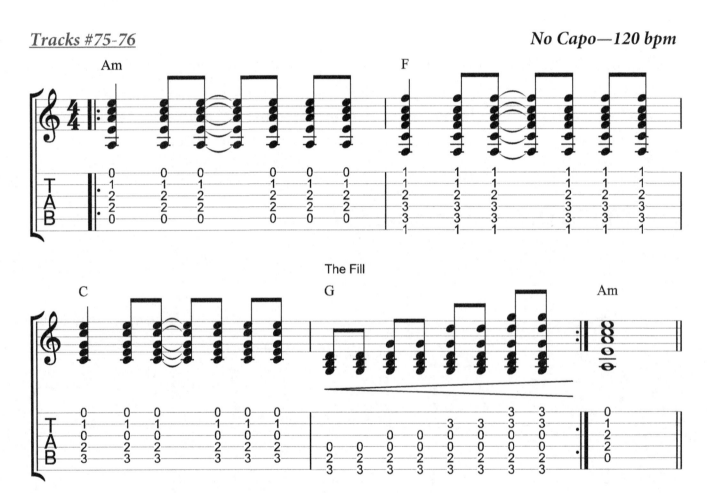

For this example, we are playing the "Ultimate" strumming pattern for the first three bars and then in bar 4 we are throwing in the strumming fill!

- Be careful not to speed up or slow down as you switch from bar 3 to bar 4.
- Play along with the audio, tap your foot, or use a click/drum beat—all will help you keep a steady tempo throughout.

The Most Intricate Strumming Fill Ever?

Ex. 2A

Tracks #77-78   *No Capo—60 bpm*

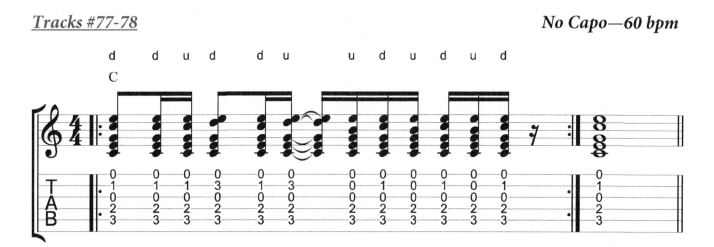

This strumming fill is a stylish one that may take a lot of practice to play. Keep listening to it to get the rhythm correct.

- Break the fill up into chunks if you need to.
- Notice the change in notes on the B string creating a melody within the fill.
- Try to follow the groove using the correct order of down and upstrums throughout if you can.

Do not worry if this fill doesn't sound perfect right away. It may take some practice. At the very least, you can use this idea to inspire your own strumming fill!

Ex. 2B

No Capo—80 bpm

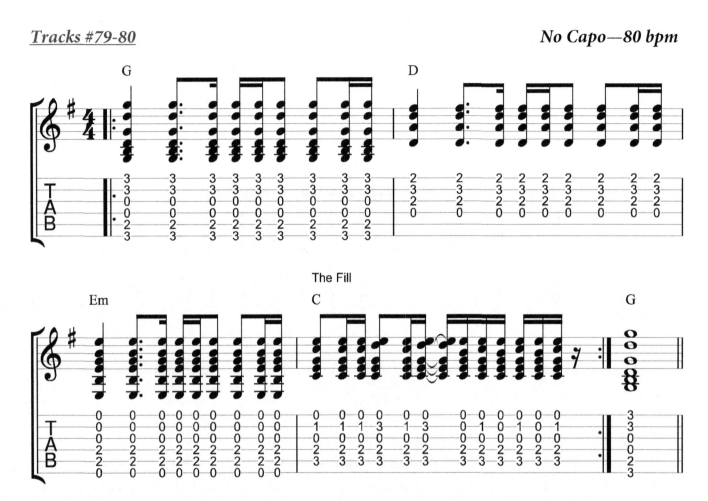

For our final example, we are using the fill you have just learnt and applying it to *chord progression #2*, and the "Modern" strumming pattern.

- Practise the first three bars on their own and practise the fill on its own as two separate sections.
- Once both sections sound good, try to merge them together smoothly.
- If you do struggle with this strumming fill, you can always substitute it for the "Build Up" strum from Ex. 1.

Remember, you don't have to play this strumming fill note for note. It is an example (and a tough one) of just what you can do when it comes to fills.

Right, that completes the intermediate section of the book. I hope you enjoyed learning those varied and exciting lessons. They are great fun. Take it steady with them and keep coming back to the lessons above. Each time you do, you will make more progress.

Before we wrap things up, there are a few more useful bonus things to learn that will help you on your strumming journey. Turn the page and let's move on...

Seven Quick Steps to Learn How to Sing and Strum at the Same Time

Every guitarist I have taught has struggled at some point with learning how to sing and strum at the same time. At first, multitasking like this can be like trying to rub your belly and pat your head! The good news though, is that with practice, you will get better at it. Here are seven steps to help you:

Step 1—Know the lyrics and the melody inside out

It goes without saying that you need to know the words and melody for the song that you are singing, really well. Learn the words and the tune inside out!

Step 2—Be able to sing the song—in tune!

If your singing is not in tune, it will likely put you off when playing (and it won't be great for the neighbours either!)

- **Record yourself singing along** to the actual recording of the song and listen back to it to make sure it sounds tuneful.
- Also, make sure the song you are singing is suitable for you. If you have a high-pitched voice like a member of the Bee Gees, it might not be too wise singing a deep Barry White song!

Step 3—Ensure your chords and strumming are perfect

Don't be sloppy with your chords and rhythm playing. Adding vocals to messy playing is a recipe for disaster. Ensure your chords are clear and your strumming is smooth—never neglect it just because you are singing. (Revisit *Part 1* of this book for more tips on this if need be).

Step 4—Keep the strumming simple

When adding the singing, you can start off by strumming the song in the simplest way possible. This can be by either strumming:

- Just one strum for each chord OR…
- Playing downstrums on each beat.

Singing over a simple strum like this can really help you get started. During the **instrumental sections** where there is no singing (such as the intro or a middle section), you can play the full strumming pattern of the song. This will allow you to show off your strumming skills—especially when you add in the techniques from *Part 3*!

When there is singing though, keep the strumming simple—especially for now.

Step 5—Work on very small sections

When learning to strum and sing, work in small chunks. Try to perfect the singing and strumming over just one line at a time or even just a few syllables. For example, for a song such as "Scarborough Fair" don't try to strum and sing the whole verse.

Instead, break it up and work on just the first bit "Are you going…",

Then when that sounds good, add in "… to Scarborough Fair" and so on.

Remember, you can break things up into the smallest chunks possible. The idea here is to get you used to strumming in a very simple manner while singing over the top of it.

Step 6—Build the Strumming Pattern Up

Next, try this:

- Build the strumming pattern up gradually by adding one strum or two strums back in at a time.

- If your rhythm is tight, you might find it easier to jump into playing the full strumming pattern.
- Try switching back and forth between a simple strum and the full strumming pattern until things "click".

Keep the singing tuneful throughout and keep experimenting. You can put the recording on and play along with it, then without it, and so on until things start to feel tight and sound good.

Step 7—Get good at singing songs that use the same strumming pattern

Here's something a lot of guitarists don't realise:

If you can sing a song that uses one strumming pattern, you may find it quite easy to sing and strum another song that uses the same pattern. It is then just a case of switching up the words, chords, and melody for the other song.

Remember, it helps if you know the song as well as possible.

The "Ultimate" and "Modern" strumming patterns are the two most popular I have come across. Therefore, it is worth making it a priority to be able to sing and strum at least **two songs** for each of these strumming patterns. As the simpler "Go-To" and "Constant Pulse" strumming patterns are easier to play, you will want to be able to do the same with these too.

There you go. That is a simple guide to learning to sing and strum.

Although the tips are simple, it takes practice to be able to master this key skill of guitar playing. The above are just a few tips that I have found have helped me and my students get good at it.

Be methodical, patient, and feel free to mix and match these tips until it "clicks". I always tell students this:

> *"Singing is a skill, guitar playing is a skill, and putting them both together is another skill. Therefore, be patient!"*

The Key "Checklists" to Use to Ensure Your Strumming Songs Always Sound Great

In this section there are two checklists you can use to help keep track of your strumming. There is a "Basic" and an "Advanced" checklist.

Each time you do any strumming, choose whichever checklist suits your current skill level and follow it. This will help you focus on the most important details when it comes to strumming and it will help ensure your strumming songs always sound as good as possible.

The "Basic" Checklist

This is the minimum you should aim for with your strumming. Everything in this checklist can be found in *Part 1* and *Part 2* of the book.

- Play all your chords so they are clear every time.
- Keep your strumming arm relaxed.
- Strum the correct strings in the chord (from the root note).
- Get clear and smooth upstrums.
- Keep a steady rhythm throughout.
- Be able to play the "Super Reliable" strumming patterns.
- Get tight at strumming the "Big Two" patterns.
- Learn a variety of the other strumming patterns and use them in your playing!

The "Advanced" Checklist

Here, you should be able to play everything on the "Basic" checklist, plus be able to do the following:

- Tap your foot to the beat as you play the song.
- Vary your strumming using one or both of the following ways:
  - With a "strumming variation".
  - With a "strumming fill" at the end of a section.
- Include the use of "dynamics" (where appropriate).
- Use one or more of the following techniques (where appropriate).
  - "Pick strumming"
  - "Embellishments"
  - "Bass riffs"
- Optional (if it suits the song):
  - "Swing"
  - "Rests"
  - "Backbeat percussive strumming"

Part 3 Summary

Let's have a recap of some of the important points from *Part 3*.

✓ **Practise each new technique on one <u>simple chord at first</u>**.

✓ <u>**Strumming variations**</u> can give any boring pattern a new lease of life.

✓ **Use dynamics** to add more depth to your strumming.

✓ **Experiment with "pick strumming"** to add some melody to a piece.

✓ **Practise using <u>swing</u>** to give your songs a unique rhythmic twist.

✓ **Use "rests"** to add energy and groove to a piece.

✓ Add excitement and melody by **embellishing your chords.**

✓ **Master "backbeat percussive strumming"** to add a huge groove to a piece of music.

✓ **Play bass riffs** and combine them with your strumming.

✓ <u>**Use "strumming fills"**</u> where appropriate to add tension and drama to your songs.

✓ **Master chord progressions #1 and #2** in this section (both are super useful).

✓ **Learning to sing and strum at the same time requires** practice and patience, just like anything else, so go slowly with it.

✓ **Use the basic and advanced checklists** to keep track of your strumming as you develop.

CONCLUSION

We have reached the end of the book, but NOT the end of your strumming journey! The techniques and concepts you have learnt here will serve you well for a long time.

I have played for many years and still use these ideas daily in my playing and will continue to do so. No doubt you will do so too. Remember, there is a whole world of fun to be had with strumming. The key thing now is that you take these ideas and run with them!

To be the best strummer you can be, remember, you need to make sure your basic technique is good, as taught in Part 1. Then, you need to fully learn the core strumming patterns from Part 2. After this, you can apply the exciting ideas from Part 3.

If you still haven't done so, I recommend you get the extras, bonuses, and audio from this link here—**rockstarpublishing.co.uk/strum**.

Keep experimenting with the ideas throughout the book. If you do so, you will have a blast with your strumming and your overall playing will be more enjoyable for it. More than anything, keep having fun with your playing and try to enjoy every second of it. Learning and improving on guitar can be tough but it is so rewarding, so stick with it and never give up!

I want to wrap it up by saying many thanks for reading and I sincerely hope that you have found this book useful.

Wishing you all the best with your guitar playing and strumming!

Dan Thorpe

ABOUT THE AUTHOR

Dan Thorpe is a guitar teacher from just outside of Birmingham (in the UK, not Alabama). He has spent many years specialising in teaching adult students who are over the age of 40, with some in their 70s and even 80s!

He has helped <u>over 120 students in one-to-one lessons</u>, more in group lessons, and many thousands via his blog, courses, and books.

After seeing the majority of self-taught (or taught elsewhere) students struggle, **Dan went on a mission to study proper, fundamental guitar technique**, learning from classical past masters to modern virtuosos, studying psychology, and researching lots of learning methods.

He continues to use these methods to help absolute beginners, advancing beginners, and intermediate guitarists learn guitar with fundamental and pain-free technique as a priority while ensuring his students <u>have more fun on the guitar!</u>

Dan has received many thousands of outstanding testimonials for his work in this area.

To find out more about Dan, you can check out his website:

Guitar Domination—a free resource for all guitarists to learn from and enjoy.

If you want to learn more about similar techniques as taught in this book, then check out the site.

Printed in Great Britain
by Amazon

39805821R00077